In the Beginning, She Was

In the Beginning, She Was

Luce Irigaray

B L O O M S B U R Y

LONDON • NEW DELHI • NEW YORK • SYDNEY

Bloomsbury Academic

An imprint of Bloomsbury Publishing Plc

50 Bedford Square   175 Fifth Avenue

London   New York

WC1B 3DP   NY 10010

UK   USA

www.bloomsbury.com

First published 2013

British Library Cataloguing-in-Publication Data

A catalogue record for this book is available from the British Library.

ISBN: HB: 978-1-4411-3507-0
PB: 978-1-4411-0637-7

Library of Congress Cataloging-in-Publication Data

Irigaray, Luce.

In the beginning, she was / Luce Irigaray.

p. cm.

Includes bibliographical references and index.

ISBN 978-1-4411-3507-0 (hardcover : alk. paper)– ISBN 978-1-4411-0637-7 (pbk. : alk. paper)– ISBN 978-1-4411-8186-2 (ebook epub : alk. paper)– ISBN 978-1-4411-9840-2 (ebook pdf : alk. paper) 1. Philosophy, French–20th century. I. Title.

B2430.I73I5 2012
194–dc23

2012012875

Typeset by Fakenham Prepress Solutions, Fakenham, Norfolk NR21 8NN

Contents

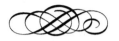

Acknowledgements

I began this book a long time ago, before the end of the twentieth century. For various reasons, I finished other books before it. However, some chapters have already been given, in earlier versions, as talks during conferences and appeared in the publication of the conferences' proceedings: 'The Ecstasy of the Between-Us' during the conference *Intermedialities* at the Erasmus University in Rotterdam in 2002 (published by Rowman and Littlefield, edited by Henk Oosterling and Ewa Plonowska Ziarek, in the series *Textures*, 2011); 'The Return' during the conference 'Luce Irigaray and "the Greeks": Genealogies of Re-reading' at Columbia University in New York in 2004 (published in *Luce Irigaray: Teaching*, Continuum 2008, and in the conference's proceedings *Rewriting Difference, Luce Irigaray and "the Greeks"*, edited by Elena Tzelepis and Athena Athanasiou, Suny Press, series *Gender Theory*, 2010); 'Between Myth and History: The Tragedy of Antigone' during the conference *Interrogating Antigone* at Trinity College in Dublin in 2006 (published by Oxford University Press, series *Classical Presences*, edited by S. E. Wilmer and Audroné Žukauskaité,

2010). These chapters were written directly in English by me and reread by Mary Green and Stephen Pluháček. The three other chapters are published for the first time. They have been translated from the French jointly by Stephen Pluháček and me.

I deeply thank all the people who contributed to the realization of this volume through their help to establish the English version of the text or the confidence they showed in my work by inviting me to give a talk, by publishing it and by allowing me to reprint it again in this book. Many thanks also to Angelika Dickmann for helping me to collect the final electronic material of the book and prepare it for publication.

1

Introduction: The ecstasy of the between-us

It is probably necessary to return to the world of the Presocratic philosophers in order to understand something about the between-us today.

Entrance to such a world takes place through a guide, a master. He initiates the disciple, a kind of son, to the truth, to the logic of Western truth.

This master often begins his teaching with the words: I say. That is to say, he considers that the truth is guaranteed by his own speech, and the disciple has to repeat the same discourse, arguing: he says, or he said. The truth is thus passed on from the master to the disciple, like from a father to a son. The truth is passed on between men, in a genealogical or hierarchical way.

The forgetting of her

We know, as, for example, Clémence Ramnoux reminds us in her work on the Presocratics,[1] that in the beginning it is a she – nature, woman, Goddess – who inspires a sage with the truth. But generally the master conceals what he received from her, thanks to which, thanks to whom, he has elaborated his discourse. He does not say very much about such a source because he lacks words or because he wants to keep it to himself – because he cannot or does not want to talk about his relationship with her. This relation thus remains hidden or removed with respect to the teaching of the Presocratic master.

However, certain masters allude to her: such as Empedocles or Parmenides, each in a different way. Even Plato hints at her, at least when it is a question of love, of the relation-between. But, in any case, they are men who evoke an absence or someone absent, a gap or a surplus. They refer to something other than their discourse, a beyond for which they have no words, and above all no logic. A something that they conceal, to which they sometimes allude in her absence. A something that will be left apart from the logos, for better or for worse.

At that time, a memory still exists of an unsaid, of a beyond in which wonder, magic, ecstasy, growth and poetry mingle,

---

[1] The works of Clémence Ramnoux to which I mainly refer are *Heraclite* (Les Belles Lettres, Paris, 1968) and *Parmènide* (Éditions du Rocher, Paris, 1979). I use a capital letter for the word Goddess as Clémence Ramnoux does in her translation of Parmenides. Commenting on the difference between the capital letter of 'Goddess' and that of 'God' would necessitate another text.

resisting the logical link that is imposed on words, on sentences, on the world. Some traces remain, at least in the discourse of certain masters.

A sort of ecstasy still exists with respect to every discourse, every exchange between men in public places or in other coteries, where they speak, they speak only between themselves. Something remains that they cannot express, nor even experience anew, lacking gestures or words to say it, to pass it on, to produce it. Only the memory of an experience lasts – which little by little will be effaced – the experience of a marvelous, inaccessible, unutterable beyond. A beyond which arose from an encounter with her – nature, woman, or Goddess – about which most of the masters say almost nothing, back to which they do not send the disciple. Their teaching ought to be self-sufficient, unrelated to her as a source.

Certainly not all the masters then claim that it would be so, but some of them do. And, little by little, their teaching will introduce the disciple into an enclosed universe, parallel to the living world, to the natural world. Nevertheless, for certain masters – like Empedocles or Parmenides – the whole of discourse is still mysteriously based starting from her – nature, woman, or Goddess – remaining the inaccessible thing from which words arise and to which they are addressed. However, for others – Heraclitus, for example – discourse closes upon itself through strategies of conflicting oppositions. Henceforth, it becomes possible that conversation and dialogue take place between oneself and oneself, within or between the same one(s), and truth and language begin to speak from themselves, on themselves, without any source in an other or return to an other, an other who is in the beginning feminine – nature, woman, or Goddess. Man settles himself in his house of language, cut off from the real and from the other as real. A tautology of words, of truth locks the speaking subjects – master and disciple – in a shelter, a universe, a logic which is intended to duplicate what belongs to their birth, their growth, their natural reality. This gesture happens in a more secret, more subtle manner than that of Prometheus, and prepares for a death through suffocation, exhaustion, isolation, conflicts, and finally destruction of her – nature, woman, or Goddess. She vanishes in a culture based on sameness, beyond which she extends, and to which the nostalgia of certain masters towards a beyond still bears witness. They allude to an 'emptiness,' a 'hole,' at best a 'Being' beyond their discourse for those, like Parmenides, who still trust her.

In fact, she doubly vanishes. In order to definitively close the logos upon itself, in order for the logos to speak with itself, the traces of a relation with her are said in the neuter. For example, *On* in the singular is used to designate the totality of beings – there is *On* – and the beings are named *onta* – there are *onta*. Instead of saying: the world is born from her, and from my relation with her, the Western philosopher says: there is Being, there are beings, which is, or are, given without anyone who gives. There is, there are, without being born in a way, without any origin. There is, there are, mysteriously there. With the neutralization of his own being and of the whole of the universe, the Presocratic philosopher somehow prepares our tradition for nihilism.

Furthermore, to compose with the neuter is not an easy task. When it remains the effect of the removal and effacing of her and of the relation with her, it is still possible to endure the neuter. But after the forgetting of this beginning, the neuter becomes what undoes the whole of the world, of any subjectivity. In fact nothing gathers together in a neutral perspective, nothing except our hatred and the belief in the higher value of neutrality with respect to a real existence. Such is the case at least in the Western tradition, which does not care about a cultivation of breathing at the service of life, thus always at work in a singular life.

A between-us on hold in the beyond

After nature or Goddess have vanished into the neuter, the place is opened for the substitution of them by a God, a God in the masculine – a God who sets his absolute entity against the fluidity of the neuter, and also the proliferation of words, of things, of gods. Thus a God, unique and in the masculine, has occupied the place of the ecstasy opened and safeguarded by her. From then on, the world is closed upon itself, and the way is prepared for the hell at work today.

The house of language has become a kind of tomb to which it is necessary to give back a semblance of life. The closure of the logos, of the world, calls for contraries, oppositions, conflicts. At the beginning, exchanges between men – sometimes inappropriately named dialogues, but which are instead pedagogical strategies, verbal joustings in courts, debates in arms – are supposed to progressively lead to truth. A truth really, or because of a pedagogical feint, to be discovered. However, when God occupies the place of the ecstasy of truth, controversies of course can exist, but not about this absolute, only about the way we apprehend or approach it. God as such remains hidden, forever taken away from our perceptions. Key of all representations, God stays remote from any appropriate representation, or presentation. Our theological controversies will not render God more or less perceptible to us, so that we could assess the status of his transcendence. He occupies a place forever removed from our debates. And the truth that he is supposed to preserve, but without any possible valuation from us, is presumed to be both sovereign and unique. Absolute. Beyond our controversies and discussions.

Alas! it is not so in the deadly battles that the followers of this unique God fight against one another. Because of these, the question of his status deserves to be asked, as well as that of his relation to life. Of what importance is death for those who have situated God beyond their present existence? Is dying then not the most sure way to join him? And is it not a question of surmounting life when such a God takes the place of the mysterious ecstasy with respect to the logos, a place left vacant by her – nature, woman, Goddess? Or when such a God is situated at the source and the end of all words, all existences, all lives? He thus closes up the opening of the unutterable experience in the relation between the master and she who inspired him – nature, woman, Goddess. And he keeps in suspension – without a possible turning back to oneself or a possible sharing with the other – the breath, the gesture, the feeling or the meaning awakened in the meeting with her, a meeting lacking ways to be expressed, passed on. Which results in an ecstasy that is to be saved through a God, to be safeguarded through a beyond, without us recognizing that it must be provided or preserved at each moment by us, without us realizing that it was to be preserved between him and her, because it arises from the between-them. This between-them is annihilated if it is appropriated by the One, the Unique – truth or God – or put into the neuter as a neither-the-one-nor-the-other and not both-the-one-and-the-other.

The positive and creative meaning of this God and this neuter would be that we today discover that he or it maintain the place of the relation with the other. Certainly not by occupying their place, monopolizing it thanks to an entity for which a capital letter, or a neuter, would act as a guarantee, but instead by favouring access to the other here present through remaining supplementary to all I know – of myself, of the world, of all – as a reserve left apart from every discourse, every logic. A God, thus, who is not only the Other – with a capital letter – who allows me to become absolutely the same as myself, because he stays beyond every present, every imperfect resemblance to myself. An Other, in such a case, who is equivalent to an absolute same, to sameness itself, that I would know only after my death, in the beyond of any life. Then he would remain just an apparent other whom I must share with others, impose on others as the sole possible place of a sharing between us. Key to all representations, such a God is also chief of group(s), of people(s), of state(s), and not that God, beyond sameness and otherness – a reserve of the relation-between, a suspension of the realization, of the incarnation of the relation between us, especially as two who are different.

The God, who occupied the ecstasy left empty by the Presocratic master, has all the predicates appropriate to the suspension of the relation with her – or Her. Most radically, he resists predication, except in a negative way. He remains without any species or genus, without any particularity. Pure substance or essence – confusing in some way the two in himself – the mistake of this God is to will him to be only of his own, and also to be named in the masculine. He thus does not apply negativity to his ecstatic substance or essence, asserting that he/it is, he/it is only, relation: between the absolute and myself, between the other and myself, between us.

A relation is never only of one's own, never appropriable by any one alone. It exists between the one and the other, produced and saved by the two. This between-two takes place in the opening of the difference between the one and the other, but it is in no way proper to the one or to the other – it arises from the two. Perhaps it is the sole place where existence becomes a substance of another kind, outside any possible appropriation. Appropriating it is impossible without destroying it.

The closure of the same

A certain God has thus enclosed within sameness what formerly corresponded to the ecstasy of a relation to the other. He retained through the immutability of his eternal self-sufficiency the frail, impermanent, inconstant existence of the relation between us. A relation that is always open, constantly evolving, never proper to the one or to the other, fruit of a present in continual creation, generation.

This relation, in a way, is also taken away from our sensible perceptions: invisible, inaudible, intangible as a relation. Nevertheless, it exists. Imperceptible, it is more present than any representation. And man has tried to seize and keep something of it by submitting it to an alleged neutral sameness. Our relation, then, becomes at best a sharing in a same imposed upon us: a same language, a same culture, a same God, and not the discovery of a sharing between us. To share something that is supposedly common between us does not yet amount to a sharing of us, between us.

A sharing of the same in sameness between those who finally have become the same ones can at times be acceptable at the level of needs but not at that of desire, unless this desire be already dead, unless it be reduced to a sharing of things. It is not yet a question of a sharing between us, a sharing of our mutual attraction or desire, in a way of a sharing of ourselves. Now, in order to have access to another era of History, the gesture we must carry out is to pass from a sharing in sameness through all kinds of objects or things – material or spiritual – to a sharing of ourselves thanks to the respect for difference between us.

Our culture is based on a sharing of the same between those who have become same. Sameness can take the form of material needs but also of cultural or spiritual needs at all levels. In such a culture, we are called to become all alike, on earth and in heaven.

There must no longer be master or slave, rich or poor, white or black, and finally no longer man or woman. This reduction of differences is planned by Western culture, especially through putting into the neuter the ecstasy which took the place of her – nature, woman, Goddess – or of the relation with her. This reduction of differences leads to a cultural deluge, to a nihilism without any possible overcoming, or to an authoritarianism or totalitarianism worse than those already known, notably because they reach the core of thinking itself and claim to be universal. In order for those who become alike not to be in conflict, a vertical authority, which gathers and governs them, is necessary. A truth or a power, exercised or passed on by a master, a chief, a leader, a God the Father, must organize from on high these people who are all the same, but whom nothing really unites.

Rules are required for managing the goods and property – material or spiritual – that people share, that gather them together, divide them, weave links between them. Goods and property make them feel alike, but also higher or lower, so that they become envious of the other, and they appropriate, exchange, pay, sell one another. They act like those pieces of the scene that the Presocratic masters have organized in an apparently self-sufficient world, starting from the same or the contrary, the more or the less, the near or the faraway. This world is presumed to meet the needs – material or spiritual – of humanity.

Within such a world, the intervals between things and between persons are already planned and subjected to calculation. There is no longer any between-us that is free, available, still silent, still alive. The subjects move on the chessboard of a closed whole. Humans make up a kind of puzzle, as is the case for the totality of the pieces of the logos. There is no longer the possibility for a real creation in human relationships, either horizontally or vertically. The spaces-between are already determined. Each one believes to be moving – as when a word occupies another place and apparently modifies the whole combination of words. In reality, the whole remains the same. Which produces an entropy in the system, an exasperation, necessary conflicts to simulate a possible evolution and, finally, a need to destroy the whole.

The closure of the world and of individuals upon themselves is due to a fear of the opening, of that which remains without limits, boundless, and is assimilated to emptiness or chaos. It corresponds in a way to that which the Greek philosophers designated as *apeiron* and tried to exclude from their world. The world, like the logos and the speaking subject, thus became enclosed and cut off from a living becoming because of a desire for mastery and a fear of opening. Because of a need for mastery which results from a fear of opening?

Man, in fact, meets with an obstacle in his becoming: he is not capable of living completeness in an open horizon. The culture that he has elaborated thanks to the logos, thanks to a language obeying a certain logic, seeks to construct a closed world at his disposal: to shelter himself, to communicate with those who are the same as himself, to act as a basis or an instrument so that he can continue building a world of his own starting from pre-existing or living being(s).

How to escape opening

In order to control the opening, man will thus take the *apeiron* into his logical economy, in particular through trying to master the negative by coupling the opposites, which in part will occupy the place of the relation between him and her. Some of these couplings are especially crucial – for example, the pair Being and not-Being which serves to hold under control in the present the opening, without pre-established limits, of becoming. Man as man cannot find or live well-being in an open horizon. Against becoming over time, against growing, man will oppose Being and not-Being in the present. The *apeiron* related to becoming is thus kept in a logical economy. It is maintained between pairs of opposites, allowing for the approach or the removal of parts of oneself or of the world, which have become movable pieces of a whole held under control. But in the opposition between Being and not-Being, the original character of the being gets lost, its relation with that which lives and, as such, becomes.

Rather than opening it to a becoming that he is not capable of entirely bringing under control, man subjects his being to the rule of the logos: Being and thinking – the same, to recall the famous equation attributed to Parmenides. Thus whoever does not think, fails to be. The living being as such fails to be. Furthermore, whoever does not think according to such a logic fails to be. The relation between living beings no longer exists, except within a same logic which is cut off from the living world.

The opposition between Being and not-Being thus gets substituted for the difference between being and becoming, being today and being differently tomorrow – but also for the difference between who I am and who the other is. Nevertheless, it is necessary to simulate a becoming, otherwise death becomes too apparent. Likewise it is necessary to simulate difference(s).

Becoming is simulated through the movement of pieces within a logical structure, as well as by the number of pieces. The whole remains finished, closed, but depending on whether the pieces gather in one way or in another, the spaces inside the whole or between the pieces become modified. Nevertheless, they are pre-established by the closure of the whole.

The logos seems to be multiple and in becoming – a sort of analogon of the living world. However, even if its pieces are numerous and if they may fragment, the growth, in such a universe, is only apparent. The proliferation of the pieces, which carries a proliferation of organizations between them, takes place in a structure that is in a way static, immutable. In this closed universe, the relations to being strangely evoke the relations of a fetus with the placenta. Human being, at least the masculine human being, is submerged in a world that he partly produces and from which he is not separable. He thus finds himself isolated, cut off from every relation outside his placenta.

Another coupling of opposites that is crucial for the relations between people is made of love and discord, a word often translated in English as 'strife'. However, 'strife' rather designates an effect of discord or hatred – to recall the word used by Clémence Ramnoux to translate 'neikos'. This pair of opposites, above all in the work of Empedocles, also bears witness to needing to control the in-between in a closed world. What is more, love and hatred are envisioned in connection with the constitution of the world rather than with the relations between persons. The two – love and hatred – are necessary. Love produces the motion of expansion and mixing, and hatred the explosion of the whole and a retreat. The pairing of love and hatred is sometimes confused with or assimilated to the pairing of whole and parts or completeness and fragmentation. In fact, it is a more complex matter because it implies the relations between the elements of the universe: water, earth, air, fire and their passing into one another.

Such a coupling, in which we still believe and which still corresponds for us to the motion of forming a unity or going back into parts, has to be questioned. The difference between love and not-love, love and the absence of love, seems to be more appropriate to the relations between persons. Love would remain what allows us to constitute a world and draw near to the other. Loving arouses an energy able to compose a whole, to secure the cohesion of a world and a subjectivity. In the absence of love, there is chaos, the destruction of subjectivity and of the world. Yet the cultivation of the relations between us requires a return to oneself which has nothing to do with hatred. An alternating motion between going towards the other and returning to oneself, of opening to the other and returning within oneself, is necessary in order to preserve the two persons. In reality, the alternation of love and hatred takes place within only one person and their own world. It does not yet represent a motion that takes into account two persons and the between-two that they must establish, maintain, cultivate. Love in the Presocratic coupling formed of love and hatred is still a part of what I consider as not-love, as an absence of love.

Another coupling of opposites that will hinder a cultivation of the between-us is the pair near and distant. The logic of Western culture ends in a substitution of representation for perception. The logos intends to create a sort of analogon of the living world. In order to succeed in that, nearness and distance have to be merged into a sole perception or representation through a ceaseless comparative evaluation, and also through naming every thing encountered. Such a denomination will substitute for a sensory and emotional meeting with the real structured into the whole of a world that man brings under control. Like Being in the work of Parmenides or even Heidegger, the names given to the real keep it, while taking it away from its status of living being. In this way, the things of the universe, and we ourselves, enter into a same world thanks to a system of denominations that governs representation, and even perception.

Such an organization of the relations with things removes us from them without any possible meeting or entering into presence. We can, in some way, have the appropriate behaviour with respect to a thing, but we do not enter into relation with it. It is no longer close to or distant from us, as is the case for the mother of Freud's little Ernst before becoming assimilated to a bobbin. How could we designate with the same word things as different as a tree with buds, with flowers, with leaves, with fruit, or a tree in spring, in summer, in autumn, in winter? How could we do that except by closing our eyes to what we see, by no longer smelling, tasting, touching? It is at the price of renouncing our present perceptions that we imagine or represent a tree through the same name.

It would be possible to say the same thing about the encounter with an other. And the matter is here so complex that we have preferred to reduce the meeting with the other to a meeting with ourselves, that is, to a meeting with someone who is supposed to share our world, our things, our language and culture. Then we have not yet approached the question of the encounter with the other as other.

A world both open and closed

Now the other is the one who can hold open the closure of the world, while providing it with limits: the other here close to me but different from myself. The relations with him, or her, keep the world, each of the worlds, both open and structured if I respect the other as irreducible to me, transcendent to me. This does not mean that the other is vertically higher than myself, as an absolute or an ideal of which I would be only one embodiment amongst others, imperfect like the others. Transcendent here signifies irreducible to myself: to I, to me, to mine.

The fact that I will never be able to completely appropriate the other and the other will never be able to completely appropriate me, maintains the subject and one's own world both open and closed. Open because the other, in their difference, remains inaccessible to me, because he, or she, represents a beyond in relation to my

I, to me, to mine, a beyond here present beside or in front of me. Closed because, through the respect for the inaccessibility, for the transcendence of the other, I subject myself and my own world to the negative in order to preserve the duality of the subjects and of the worlds in presence. This way, I and my own world are provided with limits. Contrary to its aim in Hegel's work, the negative then undoes the one, the One, and restores the two. It also preserves the place of the ecstatic interval between the one and the other, a place which belongs neither to the one nor to the other, although it is born from a relation in which the one and the other, the one to the other, are present. Such an ecstasy corresponds in part – but only in part – to the ecstasy put on hold by the Presocratic master. It does not only amount to what has been left unsaid or unaccomplished in the relation with her – nature, woman, Goddess. It also involves an intervention from him towards her – and the existence of an exchange and dialogue between the two.

Ecstasy then becomes a process in which each is safeguarded as the one who he, or she, is – with the potentials corresponding to his or her own becoming – thanks to the irreducibility between the two, the transcendence between the two, the difference between the two. Ecstasy becomes a place of, and for, desire and not only for need, which always aims to fill: the one, the other and the between-two. Desire is preserved because neither of the two can appropriate the other. Desire does not amount to an interweaving due to an unconscious proximity, a sharing of the native language or landscape, a familiarity in relation to the family house and the neighbourhood. Rather, desire means an attraction kept alive thanks to a relation attentive to the other as different from myself, thus forever remaining beyond any appropriation by myself – which allows a proximity while respecting the two, and also preserves the between-two.

Desire as such is wanting to enter into relation with the other. Desire is never wanting to possess or appropriate the other, which amounts to a real or imaginary need to reduce the other to myself or to my own. Instead it is a question of establishing, keeping and cultivating the between-us. The surplus or the beyond with respect to each one must not only end in an individual passage from instinct to culture, from a sensible immediacy to a rational behaviour, from a human nature to a divine nature. All of that ought to occur little by little without ecstasy, at least without an ecstasy that appropriates and erases the ecstasy of the between-us. This space belongs neither to the one nor to the other; it is brought forth, maintained, developed by the reciprocal attraction between the two through the respect for the transcendence of each by the other.

In order for the between-two to subsist, transcendence must be kept between the two, and not only the transcendence of the father with respect to the son, which is both too hierarchical and natural, and, furthermore, implies a becoming the same. Rather, it is a question of the transcendence of an irreducible difference between two, of which the most universal paradigm lies between man and woman, a man and a woman who are naturally different, without any similarity through blood – the sexuate transcendence between a brother and a sister keeping a share in sameness – and who affirm their cultural difference. Such a place, such a link between two is still to be created, established, thanks to the attraction between man and woman, an attraction that arises from instinct and becomes humanity and divinity.

To bring forth and to maintain the between-us as a third woven each time by the two is possible through the passage from sharing our needs to sharing our desire. The energy of attraction then enters into a psychic economy on which we can have an effect that does not amount to a simple mastery. We cannot dominate this energy, but we can transform it, we can transform ourselves. It is no longer a matter of making an object starting from a material external to us, but of constructing ourselves – not only by becoming more perfect according to already defined patterns, but by becoming more perfectly ourselves through a cultivation of the relation with the other. Which requires an alternation of being and letting be in each one and not a division of these kinds of behaviour between two subjects.

The human being as a being in relation

The philosopher must henceforth put the accent on the subject as a being in relation. Philosophy has to consider the culti-vation of our relational identity to be a decisive stage of our becoming humans. This implies recognizing that humanity is, or would be, made up of relational beings that live their relations differently from other kingdoms, especially with regard to their sexual belonging. Humanity cannot be defined as a group of individuals who assert their difference with respect to other kingdoms: animal, vegetable or mineral, through a quantitative distinction, a distinction that is founded, for example, on the number of neurons. Rather, the problem humanity must face is how to overcome the status of undifferentiated people with their necessities or needs: for food, shelter, sexuality, reproduction, leadership or servitude, and all sorts of mental appetites. It is not in a comparative way that we can reach our human being. What is more, our superiority over other species can also be that which provokes so much wandering on our part. Perhaps humanity differs from other kingdoms partly through its ability to be mistaken or to take a path that goes nowhere, or even leads it to its own extermination. This is due to the fact that human being does not simply obey necessities but enjoys a margin of liberty. Using it as a capacity for proliferation – of humans and of their productions, material or spiritual – is not sufficient for achieving humanity as such. In this case, we run the risk of becoming merely prodigal, dangerous, mad living beings, or of being subjected to our inventions, especially our technical inventions.

We must thus wonder whether our culture remains in the service of humanity or instead contributes to its destruction through a fragmentation of us into parts which are still smaller, more partial, more dead. Such a culture, then, sometimes appeals to our eyes, sometimes to our ears, sometimes speaks through words and sometimes through images, but never gathers us with all our perceptions, and never allows us to really approach one another, notably with the whole of ourselves. Which ends in a sort of neutralization, a kind of nihilism, even if it results in beautiful forms, appearances or discourses.

We must especially wonder whether technique – of which the logos is one of the first expressions – leads our humanity to its achievement or to its destruction, even if technologies can bear witness to human competences, but also to the ability of humanity to be mistaken. We must, at least, preserve a capacity for questioning our competences and productions. We must save a possibility of going back behind them in order to ask ourselves whether or not they contribute to our becoming as living beings having a certain margin of liberty.

How can we both preserve and develop our freedom as humans? It is precisely by cultivating the between-us, but not only as individuals who simply belong to a same people. In such a case, the between-us is already determined by the people and it does not remain free, still to be considered by us. Rather it is at every moment, in the relation with the one whom we are meeting, that we must cultivate the energy born thanks to this encounter. Certainly the most crucial place where we have to accomplish such a gesture is situated between man and woman working to transform their attraction into desire. Starting from desire we can do so many things, and first of all become humans, alone and together, always safeguarding the relationship between two different beings.

I have stressed the necessary consideration for the negative so that we are and we remain two, that is, so that the between-two does not merge into the multiplicity of a community. I also would like to emphasize the fact that only a general practice of art can maintain and cultivate the between-us.

Transforming our needs into desire requires the mediation of art: in our gestures, in our words, in all our ways of relating to ourselves, to the other(s), to the world. The matter is no longer of submitting, or not, art to philosophy, but of understanding that in order to reach another stage in philosophy, to promote a philosophy more appropriate for humanity as formed by beings-in-relation, we must begin by transforming our energy through a continuous artistic process. Art does not amount to a kind of unnecessary work that is suitable only for some artists. Art ought to be a basic daily undertaking carried out by everyone for passing from nature to culture, from the satisfaction of instincts to a sharing of desire, that is, for preserving and cultivating the between-us. Art is more critical than morality if we are to enter a culture of a humanity formed by beings-in-relation and not by beings supposedly of a higher capacity than beings of other kingdoms.

If we can recognize that our task is to take into account the between-us as an aspect that belongs to the core of our humanity, we will discover that, for this undertaking, art, philosophy and religion in fact are inseparable. We are then called to enter a new epoch of our human evolution, an era in which art, philosophy and religion are endowed with another meaning and put into practice in a way different from the one that we know as Westerners.

2

When life still was

The impossible mastery of natural growth

When feminine divinities even imperceptibly govern discourse, becoming still exists. Thus, in the work of Empedocles, growth and decline, rapidity and slowness qualify the movement tied up with the real, with life. Growing still takes place there, as does declining. The former is assimilated to becoming one starting from several, the latter to becoming several starting from one. At that time, silence still has the status of saying, it accompanies becoming. The world is not yet organized according to the for and the against decreed by man. A temporality is evoked there as movement towards accomplishment or annihilation, not yet fixed in frozen polarities. Life is what grows; it is not considered as a completed totality to which death is opposed.

Later life is put aside, death supplants it. With death, the grid of opposites becomes possible. Poetic language saying the plurality of the living is lost. In such a language, meaning always remained multiple but rooted in a simple, wise, and secretly religious ground. Henceforth, uprooted from this ground, it is fixed, from on high, by tables of opposites. This or that thing, this or that word will be good or bad, at best ambiguous. This logic is substituted for the exuberance of a growth of life, which nothing can stop in a definitive way. The eye ceases to look at it, the ear to pay attention to it. For an awakened perception, for contemplation, language games are substituted little by little creating in man an artificially constructed double.

To this creation corresponds a discourse uprooted from its primary function: saying the real. It claims all knowledge because it no longer belongs to life, to its secret growth, to the truth of its roots. It can say all, invent all, and thus deceive. The master leads the disciple into the infinite mazes of his skill in manipulating words and linking them together. He seduces him to the night into which he himself has entered, by scorning the sun as that which unveils what is. In this way the obscure becomes the clear through a reversal in which what frightened man – himself? – is transformed into the aim of his desire: the all knowing.

If man himself disposes of meaning, then all, at each moment, can be reversed: all he has to do is decide it to be so, and to lead the disciple to believe that it is thus. Without eyes or ears that one can trust, the paths of education are mapped out by the master for an entry into a logos at the service of whoever knows how to manipulate it.

Abandoning the mystery of life – never utterable by anyone, evoked only by the poet – grants power to the logician, However, it is at the price of having opted for death, in return for a play of words: life and death are the same, to live is to die, death is the other side of life, etc. Whoever lives outside of this logical economy would be ignorant. This means anathematizing the one who refuses to enter into our system, without wondering about the origin and the scene of the deception, and of leading the other to opt for a common path instead of searching for his or her own way.

A common meaning begins to predominate. And whoever fails to perceive it will be described as sleeping, as mad; which does not rule out that this very one in fact remains in contact with life. Yet it is without entering into the circle of those initiated into the logos, of those who are capable of hearing and speaking that coded speech which founds the community of men – leaving women to communicate by means of obscure signs, particularly in the name of a modesty which demands that all never be clearly exposed. The gods, whose language is not easily interpreted, moreover express themselves in this way.

Discord would be the opposite of love, Neikos of Aphrodite. And Empedocles, for example, has a difficult time explaining what happens between the two. Could it be because the construction is faulty? Perhaps the opposite of love would be non-love, which means energy does not exist or is not organized as such. Chaos then reigns, the uncoordinated impulses that destroy the whole. Yet there is not for all that hatred. Why couple discord or hatred

with love except in the name of a rhetoric that demands couplings
of opposites? In the name of a symmetry that philosophy needs
in order to surmount the living? Which never presents itself in a
totally symmetrical manner. To be sure, love and hatred cannot
be called symmetrical in a sense, but to lay them out at the same
level as antagonists is already too much. That, in fact, is required
by the need to substitute a *polemos*, a conflict, between entities
already artificially constructed for a movement of natual growth.
In this way the world is not motionless, it simulates life. But this
semblance is what little by little distances it from life, and allows
the logos to no longer say it, accompany it, support it.

Some evoked movements remain close to life. We are still in
the beginning .... A going outside oneself in order to go towards
the other and a withdrawing into oneself still exist. But, as soon
as mixing, indeed copulation, evoke love and the withdrawal into
self hatred, the logos will have separated the living from itself.
In order to go towards the other, to harmoniously embrace the
other, a withdrawal into oneself is necessary. It does not signify
hatred but a working out of the relation to self and to the other
with a view towards avoiding fusion, confusion, and the need for
an explosion in order for separation to take place. To simply go
towards the other, to join with the other while forgetting oneself
is not to love, but to obey an irresistible movement in which the
one and the other are dissolved.

The dissolution can be happy or unhappy: fusion and
radiance of the union in a whole or indefinite fragmentation in
separation. Everything is always to be begun again. No world can
be built in a becoming founded upon such an opposition, and

instead the one that would already exist is destroyed. The logos proves to be inadequate for saying life, and that which animates it. For assisting it in being and becoming without freezing it in models in which it no longer takes place, already reduced to a mechanism in which it has lost its roots, its sap, its growth, its blossoming. Movements which cannot be simply compared to gathering or dispersing, which instead favour seizing from the outside in comparison with an intimate becoming that it is better to let be, assisting it without any mastery.

In the beginning, the sage still listens to her – nature, Goddess, muse. They are the master, for the philosopher who begins to speak. And his discourse still grows starting from the same depths as vegetal growth. It is not yet separated from them in order to constitute a logos parallel to the living world, which says this world while cutting it off from the roots of life and its becoming, transforming it into signs so as to put it at the disposal of the works of man. Instead of looking, listening, contemplating with a view towards learning from her, from them, what is to be said, the philosopher then sets out on a path which is no longer that of wisdom but of the arrogance of a demiurge.

He forgets life: the first master, and its teaching which inspires appropriate words. Instead of searching for the place that, in him, could unite diverse perceptions, instead of safeguarding a heart attentive to life and listening to it, to them, he closes himself to her saying, to their saying, giving himself over to the construction of a world of artifice, to the elaboration of a cosmos of words in which he will lose his way, misled by his own work.

The education of the eyes, of the ears, of the heart, which makes man able to receive a teaching from her, from them, becomes an occluding that ends with the entry into a world of delusions in which the one who has barely begun to speak claims to be the master, forgetting from whom he must, first, receive a teaching.

Through the establishment of opposites, man constructs and imposes his domination. Playing at contrasting them and mixing them up: in verbal couplings that designate actions, qualities or states relative to things or to man.

Thus: 'things taken together: by wholes and by pieces'; 'turned towards one another, turned away from one another'; 'sung in harmony, each sung in its tone'; 'One from all, all from One'; 'to be present, to be absent'; 'to be nearby, to be faraway'; 'disperse and assemble'; 'holds together and goes away'; 'advances and withdraws'; etc.

The subjects of the verbs are then in the neuter: plural to designate all things, singular to say the thing par excellence, evoking a divine dimension. Sometimes the relation of things between themselves or that of man to things is told about, particularly with regard to the nearby and the faraway.

Opposites are said with regard to the same or the same ones. And, through the ambiguity arising from their designation by words, things or god maintain a semblance of life. They are same or other according to the time, the arrangement, the context of their appearing. So it is with the natural world, with its growth which always presents a new appearing.

But *phusis* is already cut off from its living roots by the logos. The multiplicity of names for things, even for god, refers to the diversity of effects that they have upon man. The eyes, ears and other sensible perceptions are closing for a mastery of the real, the contemplation of which no longer inspires the truth.

In the beginning, to perceive and to think are the same. And what man thinks is not dissociated from what is around him. The two remain linked together. Attentive to his surroundings and to the landscape in which he is situated, man receives from them the roots of his becoming. He still lives in faithfulness to her, nature or Goddess. He espouses her movement, and in this way knows her, and knows Aphrodite.

Teaching moreover cannot take place outside of she, of they, who unveil(s) the truth. Situated in her, in them, the master and his disciple(s) attempt to say what she, what they, reveal(s) to them. They strive to be present to what is present to them. As man, as men, they organize this coexistence with words. They build themselves an environment where they live in her, in them, with a language of men. This language helps them to name the present that surrounds them, but also to secure an extensive or intensive memory of it. What is said will find a place in an already perceived landscape that man remembers. In this way the nearby and the faraway are woven together. This is true in time, and it is also true in space. Thanks to his memory, man makes the past present and brings together, then confounds, what is perceived elsewhere with what he perceives here and now. A world is organized, the risk of which will be that it claims to double, while forgetting, what already is. That is especially the case if reflection upon oneself prevails over attention to the surrounding atmosphere or landscape.

The Western man in this way little by little wandered away from what surrounds him, of which he has not assured the saying. Withdrawn into himself, he has substituted a universe of representations, progressively cut off from the real, for the perception of the external world.

Enveloped within his own language

For the ancient Greeks, saying still resembled inventing the epic of an existing world, whose master will be the bard or the translator into words. The logos, at that time, still expresses an adhesion to things, an attempt to pass on their message as truth. It is to her, to them, that the master, and his disciple with him, are still listening. Wisdom is elaborated between attentive perceptions and words for naming them, to speak of them to one another, working out in this way a shareable code. There is, then, no need to believe in the words of a master whose meaning escapes you, since the attention to what surrounds and one's own memory suffice for evaluating whether the teaching is well based. Faith is in no way blind. Rather it signifies an affective and volitional disposition, a movement of adhesion of the heart to the saying of things, of the Goddess, of the master. Without such a dynamic of energy, perception of the true does not descend to take root in the body of the follower. It is not received as is suitable, and gets forgotten as soon as revealed. In order to learn, enthusiasm, friendship, obedience are necessary. A cold logic is not yet the vehicle of a knowledge that claims to be aseptic and detached from sensory experience.

Nevertheless, man encounters an obstacle in his becoming. In order to think Being, he needs to constitute a compact, indivisible, timeless unity. He cannot live completeness in the open. What grows and knows completeness in the uncompleted, is considered by him as non-Being. To a becoming in duration, he opposes Being or non-Being in the present. Creating a closed world in order to stand up and separate himself from who or what he needs, he reintroduces a play of alternations which attempts to animate this immobile, dead universe. He does his best to give rhythm to it through a scanned speech, as though it were poetry or a hymn of praise. But the words no longer adhere to the real, no longer transmit a living energy. They are pieces detached from an artificially constructed whole, a kind of puzzle of the world that man has elaborated in order to become autonomous and dominate life. He plays at putting these pieces together in various ways, experimenting in this manner with the possibility of pursuing his enterprise. Some arrangements bring the journey to a halt, others present a possibility of continuing it. The latter will be retained as wise, not necessarily in the name of a faithfulness to what already was, but because they allow mimicking the living by mastering it through a demiurgic game.

What is at stake, for man, is reconstituting a closed universe. The words used to designate the relations to Being evoke those of the fetus to the placenta: 'to be immersed in,' 'to adhere to,' 'nothing other besides' (not even, and especially, not the mother?), 'to be attached to' and evidently to receive from it what is necessary to be oneself, to think and to say. Even when it is a question of atmosphere or surroundings, it seems that the environing world is without distance, forming one body with man, bringing him vigor and truth, a sort of maternal substitute that he refuses to recognize as such.

Man does not yet seem to be born to the world, nor to be situated in a universe that welcomes him, among others, into a milieu that lives on its own life. He does not perceive the difference between his own existence and that of nature. A fortiori is he unaware of any other beside him, unless this be a master or a disciple, in search of or sunk into oblivion of a same truth, allowing them to coexist in the common: in their little bubble or the larger one of the city. In these, man looks for a divine manner of being that, as wise as it claims to be, is founded upon forgetting.

Man looks for the present, but does not find it. Too enclosed in his bubble, he cannot meet up again with what is there, before or beside him. A veil always separates him from it – a dream or a forgetting. The closure in which he is situated is projected upon the universe, all quite enclosed in the unity of a being – and Being – such an invisible mist that covers it over and draws its horizon. Soon the flower is only perceived through an idea of flower. Its present flowering no longer gives rise to contemplation thanks to the energy it gives in this way for perceiving. It recalls an image corresponding to a name. For faithfulness to this coupling, colours and scents become rather embarrassing ornaments, threatening to thwart recognition. An imperceptible film separates man from things, to which he becomes close by appropriating them in a same construction without being able, in the present, to meet them by means of his senses. All is darkened by what it is necessary to see in order to see well. The eyes no longer open, innocently, upon the surroundings.

And the signs that the gods send through things are no longer perceived. In order to trap the never univocal truth of a god, man distinguishes him into several, corresponding to the moments of appearing that he has identified. From the Goddess, omnipresent in the environment, he has made gods. These share between them the functions, the roles, at best the aspects of the living, the whole of which is no longer animated by breath. The divine has already left the world: at the disposal of man, who attempts to force the god to pronounce oracles according to the categories that he imposes upon him, beginning with 'yes or no.' But such a logic is unknown to a divinity who still represents life.

Life never speaks simply. It shows itself in its flower, hides itself in its roots. It appears and disappears according to necessities that do not obey the opposition of 'yes' or 'no.' It remains in the 'yes and no' of manifestation. Words cannot show life more than it shows itself, unless they cut it off from the sap that gives it unity. And, after having listened to the teaching of the master, man will not see more life.

It is not words that will awaken man to what the flower is. Perhaps a cultivation of energy and sensory perceptions would teach him more about it? Closer to the lived experience of the flower, he would better perceive how it exists and can blossom – not by conformity to an image or an idea but by faithfulness to a seed, an earth, a nourishment that are proper to it.

The teaching of the master moves away from such wisdom, except when occasionally it becomes listening, praising, rhythm accompanying natural growth. If not, it moves away from this growth, as a man endowed with legs that do no cease to uproot him from his native land. He thus forgets his surroundings and himself, closing his eyes and ears so as not to remember, not to be distressed, not to be burdened with faithfulness.

This forgetting corresponds to a certain sleep. Moving here and there, man does not cultivate the perception of what is, he is not attentive to the real that surrounds him. Even though awakening to his environment could nourish his life, he does not concern himself with this. He looks to discourse for a coherence that he has lost. The world is transformed into pieces of a puzzle whose whole remains an enigma to him. And the same goes for himself as well, composed henceforth of separated members, deprived of a breathing that animates the unity of the whole.

Except at times in a search for the god or for the One, indeed in the enthusiasm of wanting to grasp the truth of things. But what knowledge will correspond to the energy awakened in this way? Who or what will give it back to itself so that it feeds the body and the soul? So that it can return there, remain there, grow there?

Did not delegating growth or becoming to the logos take these away from the flower? Away from man himself? And confer on a tool, on a technique, a life they do not have? Would this not be to believe that it is possible to create with words as with the breath? Now, if breath emanates from life, it is not evident that this is always the case for the logos. And the resistance of the disciple to the expert in discourse is perhaps not simple stupidity. Why abandon the sap of life for a diet that just as easily brings death to pass? To what does the submission required by the master – who supposedly knows – lead to, given the ambiguity of his words, if not of his gestures? Why admit *a priori* that this is good and that bad, this true and that false, that it is necessary to say 'yes' to one thing and 'no' to another? What kind of reason has in this way divided the world in two, cutting it from its living roots? Requiring the disciple to believe prior to undergoing experience. Interposing between self and self the experience of an other – which stops the sap, paralyzes it, transforms it. Grafting the primitiveness of the disciple with shoots so foreign to life that the survival of the roots is far from being ensured.

To be sure the logos is not always hypostasized from life, but only on the way to being so. It is not always already parallel to the living, but most often claims to be its doubling. And how to graft the one upon the other? Can a model extrapolated from the plant take life upon this one? What type of hybridization will mixing the two generate? Which will prevail, life or semblance?

He claims to teach the true when he begins his instruction with: I say. He does not begin his discourse with: she said, even though it is she, Goddess or nature, who inspired him. In fact, he repeats or he transposes the meaning that she, or they, transmit(s). But he appropriates it and presents himself as the master of the message received in secret from her.

The breath that will animate the pronouncement of this message by the disciple, the rhythm and poetic scansion with which he will mark the recitation of the lesson he received are addressed to the master, whereas the latter received these from her. And, when he says 'from the depths of me' the true is pronounced, he has already uprooted what comes from the depths of her and what he perceived in an intimate exchange.

Henceforth, master and disciple communicate in her, but this is not said. A hierarchy of transmission is instituted whose source is silenced, and little by little covered over: what she gives to think, or at least to perceive, through a global perception in which the unity of a whole is preserved. The master will express as he can such a divine silent message – passing from lyric or poetic singing to the play of words in which, beyond contradictions, he searches to perceive the inaccessible. Whatever his choice, he conceals the first saying, that of the Goddess – or of nature – whose place he has taken.

It is however what he receives from her that he values as positive – the Thing itself. And yet what he says of it already involves a ruse or an artifice, indeed his words were not born from his own ground but from that of the Goddess.

From then on the master hunts down in the disciple a possible falsehood. But how to avoid falsehoods when the truth is no longer received from the Goddess herself? The master cannot say exactly what she transmits. He thus already effaces the source of the message, and the non-being – and non-Being – that he produces by substituting his speaking for what he perceived from her – Goddess, nature, woman. This non-saying of the difference between her and him already extrapolates the saying from its real origin. That the master claims to possess the secret of the truth and to have expressed it as well as he was able does not prevent this interpretation from already being a forgery: it is not the same breath, the same life that animates it. And what he received from her, he does not return to her. In this non-restitution to the source, being – as Being – is cut off from the real and from its truth. The truth uttered by the master is already an artifice because it does not take into account the non-being – and non-Being – that separates it from her. Without this attestation: I am not her, the master loses his way by substituting the masculine teacher for the origin of his saying, of the saying.

A world from which women, mystery, wonder withdraw

The exchange between her and him would have better unveiled what the truth really is. But the master says nothing about that. Apparently, they never speak together. He listens to the message that she transmits to him, and he speaks to his disciple who must listen to him. They are never two listening to one another and speaking to one another with respect for their differences. And what was a difference of gender between her and him merges into a difference of generation when he becomes the master of the word. Gender then changes meaning: the negation at work in the alterity between her and him is concealed by the genealogical ascendance of/and the teaching of the master.

From then on discourse becomes the speech of the man who wanders. And the more the logos gains in value, the more the function of speaking in fact loses value.

In whatever way the masters will try to measure themselves or be measured against an other who would be closest to the truth, all of them are already uprooted from the truth, because it is from her – or Her – that they have originally received thinking. And, if they do not relate to her, to them, what can they still say? Perhaps they name a world already in the past, without life. They call knowledge what has already deserted loving thinking, what has exorcised the inspiration coming from her.

The master forgets the relation of thought to love. He reduces it to an acting without saying. An acting that even ignores the suspense, the withdrawal, the: it is not me who is the source of the truth that I utter. This truth was breathed to me by an other that I do not know, of whose knowledge I am unaware.

For lack of proclaiming that she is at the very origin, she recedes into darkness. Henceforth man creates a logos already foreign to saying. He constructs discourse by resorting to diverse strategies. The most radical will be: 'it is' or 'it is not' – meaning: in his world. This declaration, in fact, rests on a ground of non-said: it is the difference between her and him that has inspired the first words. The logos is founded upon a silenced being – and Being. Being that henceforth appears, is recognized, belongs to the discourse of man, to his own acting, his own creation. In this fabrication of meaning something is concealed that he sometimes strives to name without truly succeeding: void, hole, One …. The most faithful to her – or Her – speaks of Being.

Some still perceive the absence of some thing – or of some one – that they pursue without being able to guess the nature of what – or of whom – it is a question. Those who apply themselves to wisdom say that all flows, same and different, ultimately from an enigma. They strive to sense something of this, to be faithful to it without ever reaching it or being able to name it. This faithfulness supports the coherence of their propositions. An original silence underlies the noise of their words. While one who still relates to her – or Her – knows the silence in speech itself.

In what she passes on, meaning remains a mystery. But if it is welcomed with trust and reverence in the depths of the self, it bears fruit, provided it be allowed to take root and grow without wanting to appropriate it, to make it one's own. Which amounts to removing it from the real that gave rise to it and the interiority that welcomed it – from then on frozen in artifice, dead.

This message cannot be openly shared in the city. It requires the intimacy of a heart, a home, a sanctuary. A natural place can serve as a site for such a meeting, a silent place, foreign to the intellectual conversations or idle chatter taking place in public spaces or other coteries. Rumour does not let its word be heard here, nor let the discretion of some of its gestures be perceived.

In her absence, they all speak of the same thing, arguing about a common ground accessible in broad daylight. They make a lot of noise and, alone, the words transmitted from mouth to ear allude to her. But generally they are without reverence or respect. And it is somewhat in spite of them that they are compelled to pitch their voices lower, to adopt a hushed voice, often accompanied by loud laughter.

Apart from these private conversations, they remain together, all men, exchanging information of a general order. The words or formulas that they use are already coded. They repeat in a way the names or phrases supposedly suitable for everything that happens. They persuade one another that 'it happened again,' that 'the same thing has occurred' under somewhat different modalities, that they have recognized and adequately reported it, that what they say of it is true because it is correctly named.

In this urban unrest, repetitive and without becoming, men gather together and make themselves men – far from her, or Her, and from the gods.

From the moment they separate from her, or Her, they also distance themselves from the gods. They want to be men and to teach their sons to be men. One of the tools that they forge for this becoming is a discourse of between-men.

Little by little the inspiration that the first speaking man received from her will be sealed off by means of arguing without ever leaving discourse itself. Skillfulness in reasoning supplants wonder and trust in listening to the other. One converses between men while proving to oneself that the possibility of doing this has been henceforth acquired. Man becomes the lord of the public place. Women are in the house and the gods are in the sanctuary. On one side nature, on the other the divine, both guardians of the heart and of memory. And him, between the two, inventing a new world – the West.

This world will be constructed from a know-how, at the level of discourse and work, which presupposes an apprenticeship and appropriate techniques. And it is to the elaboration of these that man henceforth devotes himself. The foundation of his ethics becomes effectiveness: demonstrating that one is capable of building a world, one's own world, and all by oneself – without listening to what she says, or to the will of the gods. He even creates ways of questioning oracles so that they respond to him in accordance with what he, man, wills.

He no longer has much time to experience what already is, the natural world, for example. Of that beginning, he retains in himself a sort of interiority that, for lack of words and listening to her, or Her, wastes away. Unless it is transformed into effects of discourse and intuitions dictated by the work of arranging words. It is to this undertaking that the wisest devote themselves.

Instead of cultivating the energy awakened by her, of transforming the enthusiasm and wonder that she has aroused, man plays with words. He divides the whole into parts that he separates or draws together in order to create meaning. The division into two corresponds to a basic strategy. The two that he formed with her becomes an opposition of categories: being/Being and non-being/non-Being, awakened and asleep, day and night, life and death, etc. A dualism invented by him, differing from the duality existing from the beginning, which he trains himself to master, accenting or annulling the opposition.

Rather than setting out in search of an energy suitable for her – or Her – and him, he closes his world, and gives rise to movements through games of division and drawing together. Moreover, he asserts that the same and its opposite are in some way one – or One. Except for Being and non-Being, an opposition which, secretly, recalls Her? All the rest is henceforth part of his construction. And, in this construction, everything ultimately amounts to the same, including the elements of the universe that pass into one another so as to keep the whole immutable. He invents a world without change, a mechanism with neither life nor breath. The maintenance of homeostasis is already at work, which contributes to the closure of his universe. To be sure, at each moment the mechanism is in movement, but it assures the permanence of the same, to the detriment of becoming. An illusion of life is created, of which he is the master.

From this world women and the gods have withdrawn. They no longer inspire words, no longer participate in conversation. The religious domain is displaced into a speaking between men. And, first of all, into the teaching of the master. The hierarchy between the one who supposedly knows and the disciple retains something of a ritual, even of an initiation. But what constituted the divine character of the mystery has withdrawn from them.

In the mystery there still exists a flesh that cannot express itself in a distinct and reasoned way. Gestures, songs, poems try to approach it, suggest its existence, even give rise to its presence. It is sensed, perceived, sometimes indirectly exalted. But nothing about it can be said in the form of a 'it is this' or 'it is that.' Rather it is ceaselessly necessary to repeat: 'it is not this,' or 'it is not that.' Until one stops at an irreducible: 'it is,' which it is advisable to commemorate without ever being able to name it in a clear and univocal manner. This being – or Being – cannot be mastered, no logos can signify it as such: it stays above or beyond. And when men converse between themselves, it vanishes. Ritual, from then on, becomes formal and the truth dogmatic. The heart and memory little by little abandon them, enthusiasm and trust fade away.

There remains only a mental agility that plays at assembling and separating words in order to construct a world that life, love, flesh have deserted. Man plays alone, or with his fellow men. And, gradually, he forgets to pay attention to the mystery of the other, and to the relation with her – or Her.

A logical dualism supplants a natural duality

Mystery becomes ambiguity. It is no longer flesh but an effect of language. Meaning is not univocal, to be sure, but equivocation is the work of the logos and of its mastery or non-mastery by man. It does not signify a presence that cannot be seized by discourse. What was a manifestation of the irreducibility of the other – of her or Her – becomes creation of man. He invents this means for testing the intelligence of the disciple, indeed even of the gods.

Which meaning will be chosen from among the diversity of those that are possible? What does it reveal about the profundity of 'soul' or the 'wealth of treasure,' of the candidate for wisdom? And about the perspicacity of the god vis-à-vis the skillfulness of man in dissimulating? The master sets traps with his new plaything, the logos, and he watches. He no longer listens, religiously, to the message transmitted by her, nor even by the gods. He lies in wait for the reactions of the speaking or knowing apprentice. What he looks out for in this way is just as much his own competence.

Confrontation is displaced from the ability to handle weapons to that of handling words, sentences. Conflict spreads. Every relation becomes an evaluation of know-how, in which antagonism is more or less open or masked. Artifice is substituted for mystery in the relations between belligerents. All blows are permitted provided that the Wise Thing is kept in view, the inaccessible absolute neuter of which nothing can be predicated. It is fitting to tend towards it without ever reaching it or knowing anything of it.

Except that it stays beyond all that is known. It occupies the place of the mystery of the other – Her, but also her, them – whose passage to the neuter has taken away the flesh. Absolute, not because of its irreducible alterity but because of an extrapolation in which it remains suspended, inaccessible in the world of man. She no longer is – the Wise Thing is a substitute for her, the Unique One that the arrow of clever words aims at without ever hitting. How could it still be reached as a mere place or an effect of substitution, both in the target and in the means? A deception is nothing but an illusion that no arrow can ever penetrate.

In an imperceptible reversal, being – as Being – has been confided to what effaces its origin. And what was a positive gift from her becomes the indefinite withdrawal of what has taken her place. The inability to cultivate the enthusiasm and trust that animated the relation to her – or Her – is transformed into indefinitely repeated attempts to reach an unreachable target. He does not remember Her, her, or them; nor does he educate the desire and love that she has, or that they have, awakened in him.

There remains, endlessly, an ideal of inaccessible, evanescent wisdom, that can end in nothingness.... Except as a blind artifice resulting from a dissimulation, and which resists, and even increases its consistency, as long as the delusion is not unveiled. A delusion that henceforth undermines the whole construction: life and death are the same here, and no formula proves to be definitively better than any other.

Meaning is no longer anchored in the real: it slips, the same and different, changing from one moment to the next, from one speaking to another, and yet is permanent, or at least apparently so. Rooted in a truth that conceals itself and starting from which it secretly pours forth without this being referred to it, meaning little by little loses its flesh, its sap, its content. Word is more and more empty of all signification, simple form that man strives to halt in its flow towards an undifferentiated deluge by opposing an other to it: creation of a counter-current that does not return to the source. But the energy, at best neuter, born of this antagonism does not restore life to the word. Instead it assimilates it to a category, whose relation to the real fades to the point of becoming the same as its contrary.

Man constructs a new dwelling with language. But who will inhabit it? Have the flesh, the soul not disappeared in the construction: used in order to build and, then, forgotten in this new mode of existing? From which heart and breath withdraw. And, more generally, what lives and grows.

From then on the meaning of a word is no longer evaluated according to its faithfulness to the living real or to the other, but to its occurrences in the whole of speech. The master codes his discourse, encrypts it, tries to capture the enigma in its concatenation. He wants in some way to be an oracle – not of the god or the Goddess but of a new wisdom. In fact, of himself?

He often situates the enigma between linked opposites. Progressively transferring his differences from her – or Her – , or from the god, into the logos, hardening them in order to make himself a man. What he wants to neglect or forget as mystery is displaced there. He observes or tests the consistence or evanescence of this process by opposing words, symbols, sentences, and by reducing or augmenting the space so opened. He plays at creating a world, at creating his world, at recreating the world with words, formulas and their arrangement, their punctuation. He does not mimic the world into which he was born, at least not consciously; he elaborates another one that he can master. But no direct path leads to this world, no visible door gives access to it, no way out permits emerging from it. It is a matter of entering, and above all introducing, into a labyrinth that definitively isolates you from the real, and from the other. Apparently this universe respects choices – there exist crossroads, for example – but they are predetermined. Once you have entered into this maze of meaning, it is impossible both to take your bearings and to get out of it. You are definitively trapped in the logos, arrested in your becoming.

The Wise Thing would be what still attracts you, inspires you, but as a reality extrapolatable from your world, which underlies your wandering in proportion to your forgetting of her, and of her reconstruction or substitution by you. The nostalgia that you still have for her – or Her – allows neither a return nor an access to what or whom she really is. You are separated from her by the constructedness of your world, which has used and covered over the source of the energy born from the relation with her – or Her. From then on, the origin, and the way out, are lost. Words are no longer blank stones nor are they bridges marking out a path that permits a return. Their truth and their mystery have abandoned them. Indefinitely substitutable for one another, they are pieces of a game, the one that the first speaker, the teacher, claims to master, but of which he is the hostage as soon as a word is pronounced.

Words never truly express the reality of things. And the appreciation of their truth is better revealed in the dialogue with the other – with her, or Her – in the questioning exchange with the one who inspires desire and meaning. Wanting to say, only by himself, things, or The Thing, is, for man, to become indefinitely estranged from them. To try to speak with the other represents a means of approaching them without ever adapting them to or into a world of one's own. The duality of meaning, corresponding to two different worlds, is what reopens a closure that the tension between opposites within only one world had sealed. At each moment the relation between things and words, always approximate and unstable, is then elaborated or re-elaborated.

In the difference of perspectives between man and the other, things still let their meaning be glimpsed, while keeping a part of their mystery. Linked to the flesh of the one and to that of the other, words, in their being heard and spoken, are impregnated with a non-saying, a non-sayable, also created by the relation between the two. Elaborated from the presence of each one, attentive to this presence and affected by it, their organization is not univocally definable by the one or by the other on pain of their understanding becoming impossible.

No master can decide on either the choice or the concatenation of words and phrases prior to the maturation of a dialogue with the other, unless this dialogue is devoid of its present reality and of that of the partners in the exchange. Now this happens as soon as the dialogue becomes the transmission of a meaning from a master to a disciple.

In such a gesture, the link between things and words is already in the past. Speech is the repetition of a meaning established by one alone, but supposedly common. It is no longer a present production, resulting from the encounter between him and her – or Her. Speech no longer expresses presence in the present. It repeats what he perceived and rendered into words of a past event, transmitted as teaching – by him, of him.

Only her presence would give back life and truth to the saying, and not an infinite-indefinite substitution by common words, inspired by her flesh but forgetful of her. Words that have become mediations between men, which they claim to master in order to organize their public exchanges. They are neuter, aseptic words in proportion to her disappearance but under which simmer unrecognized passions, latent conflicts and wars. And sometimes they will break out, exceeding the verbal sparring of the praetorium.

Standing out at war or at court is henceforth, for man, the means to manifest the divine. Whereas the radiated with the desire inspired by her – or Her – he is now sparkling with the brilliance of a strength capable of defeating the other – by arms or by argumentation. The potential of desire has become an aptitude for wounding and killing the adversary. Lacking words that would convey the flesh between him and her, her and him, energy becomes force. It cuts up – the world, bodies, discourses. It dominates and orders instead of exchanging. The quest for glory obtained through struggle awakens it, keeps it alive, and not the quest for a shared flowering of desire, of love.

Energy is already separated from the becoming of the flesh. It wanders, expelled from its place. It withers, searching for someone in which to be incarnated in order to survive. It is no longer experienced as such, awaiting from the masses a recognition that allows it to live on. It intensifies to be glorified. It is imposed by violence, explosion.

Man no longer listens to the Goddess, no longer exchanges with Her. He breaks the bond with Her – or her. But also with himself. He was born from her, and became starting from her. He forgets this origin of life, of his first energy: no longer singing her, no longer saying her. They might celebrate it between themselves, but instead they exchange artificially coded words, extraneous to the flesh, to her, to them.

In order to be common, words are more or less arbitrary in relation to the experienced real. They designate things or facts that are supposedly the same for all, always the same in time and even in space, immutable. Words themselves become things that pass from mouth to ear, almost from hand to hand. Life comes to a standstill, frozen in its representation in quasi-objects. And senses close to sensible, fleshly perception. Eyes and ears recognize what is seen or heard, but they no longer perceive what, of the named real, appears to them in the present.

Men no longer see or hear life or the becoming of what exists. They repeat, actively or passively, communicate with themselves or with others by means of signs presumed to duplicate the real. Enraptured in this timeless truth, they soar above or get angry, gradually losing the way to life, to themselves, to others. Sometimes they imagine that, in the beyond, the true life will come to pass. The life from which they cut themselves off by instituting a meaning parallel to the living?

3

A being created without regard for his being born

Engendered by two who are different, he confronts opposites

Cut off from her – or Her – men withdraw from themselves. They wander deprived of vigor, of energy. Animated by a mechanism as arbitrary as their language, they learn with a master how to adapt themselves to it, without failure, without errors: a false gesture, a false word or concatenation of words. They are initiated into repeating, into imitating. This apprenticeship is supposed to make them men. Instead it exiles them from themselves – and from her or Her, to whom they no longer listen, they have never spoken.

They have not found the words to speak to her – or Her – to say what they received from her, from them, and what they offered in return. They have not cultivated silence in order to still listen to her, and to prepare a place where she could utter her own words. The exchange between her and him is lacking as an origin of speech, of its meaning.

In this place, a void, a hole – for some, Being. A Being that the master appropriates in order to elaborate his logic. To be, to think and to say become the same for him, or for his disciples. The question of their double origin does not arise. Being, thinking and saying would be only one, and would amount to the same, in the forgetting of the two founding them. This initial lack of comprehension brings about an opaqueness or a mystery with regard to Being. Now a guarantee for a psyche peculiar to man, now a quasi entity hypostasized from the real and through which the world is perceived and gathered, and sometimes a place of memory of her, of them – and Her. Suspension of a becoming of the relation between him and her, Being is imperceptible, unnamable, undesignatable as such. It is. Among other things, a place of forgetting of the other – or the Other? – in which the logos of man secures himself an autonomy and a demiurgic power with regard to birth, life and becoming of everything. A substitute for her, but also for a relation between him and her, Being is perceived either as carnal or as opposed to the flesh – sometimes more substance, sometimes more essence, more content or more form. What is important is that it be, concealing in this way a negative – a non-Being – necessary for maintaining the difference between her and him.

The human species is composed of two genders. Originally, the Greek word *genos* signified both gender and generation. This second meaning perhaps resulted from the first, but strangely it supplanted and in a way effaced it. Generation, possible thanks to gender, has become that in which the importance of gender is forgotten, and what gender presupposes as duality and the negative necessary for its preservation. That the one is not the other, and that this non-Being between them is a source of relations in difference, is still unrecognized. Only natural engendering is spoken of with regard to gender, and the two genders have in this way merged into a lack of differentiation. The cultural fecundity of the meeting between man and woman has remained unknown. This place, in which a real beyond the dichotomy Being/non-Being could spring, has been neglected. It has been extrapolated into God, the origin of all that is? Or into a being – or a Being – engendered by the logos of only one? God and the logos being one and somehow the same for some, but differing for others.

The divine likened to Being is, originally, related to the Goddess – to Her – and to what the sage experiences in a meeting with Her. At that time, the gods are in the plural, She is in the singular. And Being still stands in the relation to Her – and to her.

And yet man will take over the one – the One – that she represented for him and make of it the foundation and end of his logos. With this gesture, he expropriates the world from the divine. And he enters into a universe in which truth is the result of a construction elaborated and taught by the master. Truth is no longer received by each one, even if in a way that is difficult to express through words, and that poetry alone can celebrate or sing. Truth conceals itself, unattainable beyond the origin, still underlying the journey and the aim for some, forgotten by others, for whom it depends on skillfulness in mastering a technique.

Truth, at one time perceived in the attentive and awakened meeting with Her or her – or them – now results from logical manipulations that produce more or less good effects. What matters is to be able to continue advancing in a labyrinth, to be able to simulate a movement, a change, by jumping from yes to no, from more to less, from near to far, etc. Both being gathered in a Whole whose outlets are definitively defined. Only different configurations of words modify the space or spacing of it in an unchanging logical structure, opening up new paths and giving the illusion of progress, of becoming. Nevertheless, the framework and the code are already established, taking root in what they want to deny of the beginning by substituting themselves for it. The One is fixed, excluding the other as non-Being.

The One is founded through suspending or reversing the bond of dependence upon the other. Man henceforth pretends to give birth to what is, accepting to receive the revelation of this ability from a master. It is the first speaker of the logos who says: 'it is' or 'it is not,' and who transmits this knowledge to his disciple. What is or what is not comes from the decision of an expert in words.

Speech wanders progressively away from the real in order to say the non-born, the true from time immemorial, being – or Being. So that it could be transmitted, it is cut off from what inspired it, in the beginning. It recurs outside of the place where its saying originates. It forgets what it received from her, from them, or Her. It becomes a talisman that is passed from master to disciple(s), between men. A man listens to and initiates himself into repeating the speech of another man. They remain between themselves. She is no longer there – nature, woman, Goddess.

No doubt, some masters still say that it is advisable to observe what lies in the surroundings and to try to express it according to the code that has been taught. But what is perceived is recognized and named with words that are already there. What is met in the present does not modify the saying – it is already said. The first speaker has already taught: 'it is' or 'it is not', 'it is this' or 'it is that'.

Repeat what you have heard from me, says the master to his disciple. This speech is universally valid. Wherever you go, to whomever you speak, it remains the same. Become its servant. Neither add to nor subtract from it, this speech designating what is. Your passions, your appetites and enthusiasms must from now on give way before the discourse that is taught. Your body, your flesh, your heart are very little in the face of its truth. And it is fitting that your eyes and your ears perceive the real in accordance with the words already pronounced about it. It is through a logical net that you must approach and dominate the whole and even yourself.

There where you were engendered by two who are different, you are to produce meaning by juxtaposing opposites. It is and it is not, it is beautiful and it is bad, it is nearby and it is faraway, here and there, one and multiple, together and separated.... Master becoming, master growth through playing with words. In the real, there are no opposites. Forge them in order to master what exists before you. Cover over the living with your delusions. Oppose your constructions to it instead of looking at or listening to what it is before you, without you. Substitute for its multiple composition, obeying diverse necessities, singular beginnings, a universe obeying what you imagine it to be. Setting outside all that is foreign to it, all that is foreign to you. Imagining yourself to grow when you are alone, unique, identical, the same, and to waste away when you are two. To become from then on amounts to excluding the other, and to regress to mingling with him – or her.

Such a growth is already cut off from its birth from flesh, from desires. It is already deprived of sap, of living energy, already destined to die.

Perhaps this path was the one that man wanted to take in order to escape his corporeal coming into the world, in order to ascend to the summit of himself. But it is too simple, too artificial to realize such a plan. This way claims to master the mind without having modified the energy that animates it. It cuts the head from the living body and transforms it into a repetitive, mimetic mechanism. Instead of leading the disciple to constantly question what is already known in order to awaken to what happens in the present, the master enjoins him, under the threat of rejection or exclusion from the community, to confine himself to what is taught to him. The names and the order in which they are pronounced must be respected. Whoever does not succeed in doing this, whoever remains close to life in spite of the logos, is declared mentally incompetent, or mad. That one is, in some way, expelled from the public universe of a between-men obeying laws that are in part arbitrary and hostile to whoever does not submit to them. Those who do not profit from the teaching of the master and who continue to perceive and to do outside of the saying that has been taught, without doubling and enclosing the real with words, are excluded from the community of sages, from the community of men. They are 'others,' those who remain in non-Being – singular ones outside of the common, idiots in a way.

Man enters into a world of reciprocal exchange in the quasi-commercial sense. A common money is thus imperative as is the idea of generalized compensatory exchanges, between men but also between elements. From then on it is a question of exchanging one thing with another more than of exchanging with someone. In this sense, water exchanges with fire which exchanges with earth which exchanges with air. It is a matter of calculating quantities and proportions in such a way that every-thing finally comes down to the same, without any becoming other than an apparent one. This would be true at the level of *phusis,* but also at that of the speech of man or between-men.

Man reproduces *phusis*, or at least he tries to, by encircling it with his saying. But natural growth is without limits, in the present anyway, and he cannot, in the logos, signify that *apeiron* which does not amount to a lack of limits. The plant appears with borders, with a form, but to express it as such amounts to having already deprived this plant of its vegetal life. Indeed its form is never definitive: it evolves according to the hour, the day, the season, the year. These changes are often accompanied by mutations of colour, even of odour. The word, for its part, remains unchanging, incapable of reproducing life. It arrests life in an image, an idea, which evokes life without saying it.

The same goes for a human being. It changes from one moment to the next, all the more so since it evolves not only as a body but also as spirit, which makes its mobility more rapid and more complex. Unless it freezes in accordance with the models imposed on it, the imitation of what it learns or what it encounters. Paralyzed in its becoming. Cut off from life, from its growth.

Man is then deprived of his vital energy but also of that which arises, at each moment, from the encounter with the world and especially with the other, or others. An energy that cannot be fixed in a single and definitive form, and that decreases or increases according to whether the relation with the world, with the other, is cultivated. A thing that the logos fails to do, leaving to naturalness what belongs to life itself and also to the most human of the human. The logos does not take into account the relationship with her, which, in man, can evolve from elementary vitality to a culture of listening, of speech, of love, of thought – a culture of the relation with the other, no doubt the dimension most specific to humanity.

Such a dimension will be taken into consideration only in its collective aspect, and in fact, remains tied to animality. A community needs rules in order to continue, and the human group generally contents itself with such rules. The relations between persons are subordinated to an order imposed from outside that combines with a remainder of collective and individual animality. This is especially the case when it is a matter of attraction between the sexes.

The alternation between the limit and the unlimited

Imagined to be the tool that differentiates the human species, language does not accomplish this task as long as it does not develop its dialogical possibilities. As long as it serves to appropriate and dominate the real, it is not truly distinguished from a tool that an animal might use to procure its food. Do the complexity of the tool or the mental nature of the food that is sought suffice to differentiate the human as such? It is far from evident. Does not differing from the animal world happen instead through the acceptance of appropriate limits and the assumption of the negative that the relations with the other recognized as other impose? Such behaviour – perhaps specific to a human being – requires a relation to speech and to silence with which we are still unfamiliar. We have learned to use words to name the world, and even the other, and thus to appropriate them. Yielding speech to what, or to whom, we have designated by names, listening in silence to a saying different from ours and which questions us about what we think we are or know, this gesture often remains unknown to us. At best, we expect from the other that they teach us a better way to appropriate the world and things, and we accept that the other be our master if his teachings transmit to us tools more efficient in mastering the real. This is not yet to recognize that what is most human takes place in a meeting beyond all mastery of the other and speech, because speech also arises in the exchange with the other. An already existing, already coded, tool cannot regulate listening to one another nor the appropriateness of speech that will be addressed to the one or to the other after such a listening.

If saying confines itself to naming things with a view towards ensuring a common memory and a common sharing, the event of meeting in the present between two different humans cannot occur. Their exchange is already determined by a language that does not grant to dialogue a decisive place in human becoming, and it, then, amounts to instinctive behaviours or to a participation in a common saying. Difference is necessarily excluded from it – as is singularity, except the singularity connected with the impact of the environment upon speech. But this current aspect of the exchange is already defined inside and by a discourse that claims to be timeless.

Henceforth, it is only a matter of substituting certain words for others in an unchanged syntactic or logical configuration. Anything novel and irreducible that could happen in the encounter between two human beings is, from the beginning, excluded from the logos. Now it is in this encounter that what identifies man as such takes place, as well as his ability to distinguish himself from a predator: of food, of territories, of females, of tools, of ideas. As long as language remains a tool for appropriating the world and others, it fails to truly differ from the diverse strategies to which parasites and predators have recourse. It increases the power of man in and upon nature. It augments, in space and time, his capacity to appropriate what does not belong to humanity.

Such a faculty entails reverses for man: losing his way in the search for new goods. He forgets thus what or who he is, as human, and becomes pure predation, pure appropriation. Pushing this gesture to the extreme, he ends up forsaking the living being that he is, sacrificing it to his will to possess. He uses his mental surplus, his additional neurons in order to go beyond animal behaviour, subduing and consuming still more, at the risk of his life. Never satisfied with what he needs, he picks or kills not only to eat but wastes, in his excesses, the reserves of the earth, of life itself. He safeguards, in this misjudgement, the instrument of his own destruction more than the means for growth.

This risk does not appear at once, but it can be discerned in his estrangement from her, from them, from those who give life, both natural and spiritual. It can also be perceived in his taste for measuring himself against other men, in an oratorical contest or a confrontation with weapons. A thing that does not foster life but expends it in bursts that do not endure – a brilliance which will occasionally evoke a divinity. But of what divine is this the appearance? In what way is it already an expression of the sacrifice of man to a part of him that cuts him off from his resources of life, interrupts his growth? Because he does not place his limit and his unlimited where they should be placed: his belonging to only one gender of the human species, and his being confronted with the unlimited as a living and desiring being. Which imposes the safeguard of a virgin space where the negative and the positive interact – a not appropriating for oneself so as to be able to receive from or commune with without denying oneself.

To respect the other as other would be the way to resolve such a necessity. The difference of gender is the place where limit and non-limit can be guarded. Not representing the whole of the human species gives to the subject a measure which preserves the opening of the unlimited for what happens as a result of being two. The limit and the unlimited do not belong to the same time of the constitution of the subject: the one is required for remaining oneself or returning to oneself, the other for opening to the other and welcoming a becoming received from or constructed with the other. These gestures combine staying in oneself with not confining oneself to this withdrawal, to this closure. They demand an opening and a turning to oneself, not imposed by consumption or appropriation. Rather it is a certain renouncement that determines the rhythm of their alternation: that of extending indefinitely the pretension of wanting to be the whole, of making the other one's own.

In order to differ from that of other species, human becoming needs a renouncement which preserves in the subject an emptiness, a free space for the future. This emptiness is not a lack or privation of some thing. It corresponds to an availability, notably of breath, for going beyond the past and the present. Virgin in a sense would be a fitting attribute for it, if the word signifies safeguarding a space-time for what has yet to come. The word virginity then designates a conquest rather than a given, something received from birth, that we ought to keep. Perhaps it designates what, in humanity, would be most properly human. Giving up the status of being that a certain God has assumed, virginity would maintain in a subject, woman or man, a place that nothing and no one could occupy or fill: a place saved for a future, especially in the relation with the other, without any reduction of this other to an object.

A desire that only aims at appropriation or possession does not respect the alternation between the limit and the unlimited. But is it really a question of desire in such a case? Or only of need? To keep desire living as desire presupposes that it remain unsatisfied in its instinctive part requiring satisfaction. Between need and the will to appropriate and retain things, thanks to the logos in particular, man has forgotten a cultivation of the desire proper to human being. He does not know how to take care of the fire so that attraction for the other continues to provide him with energy for his becoming. What is inaccessible and non-appropriable of the other as other preserves the fire thanks to a without-limit in which the subject does not fade away but instead nourishes his will to become.

Perhaps only human being experiences desire for the unlimited as such. However, by fixing it upon some object, be it transcendent or transcendental, man has kept it in abeyance without cultivating its living becoming. Desire, which seemed specifically human, has been deferred to the beyond, to a future that is unattainable and is to be maintained as such. To preserve without realizing, without embodying should be our task regarding desire. Consequently it is reserved for some Absolute or God, without maturation or fulfillment here and now with the other.

If the relation to the divine is not combined with the relation to the other, it might paralyze desire, the fire that animates becoming. It might congeal and even destroy the soul as a living place, transforming it into a communal reserve of precepts that arrest the growth of the human being through principles external to its singular lived experience. The cultural and the spiritual are from then on without life, without breath, without vigor – just like their medium, the logos. Imposing their general and timeless rules, they channel vital energy but do not maintain it, transform it, or educate it for a proper becoming in the relation with the other. Energy, desire are not fitted properly to a relational dimension that nevertheless is specific to a human being. And it is only at the price of their sacrifice or abandon to a general order that humans will exchange by means of a logical economy that fails to take into account the particularity of the between-them. The creation of words and gestures essential for this exchange is supplanted by a saying that is identical for all, a saying in some way public, unsuitable for dialogue. What humans can then communicate to one another are word-things that have already been defined in other contexts and are unable to express themselves and their present desire. This desire is left uncultivated and instinctive, left to what a supposedly private life conceals of both a not yet human naturalness and a secret longing for a divine that feeds the attraction carrying towards one another those who are in love.

At that time, the link between desire and the divine is still alive. And it first manifests itself between him and her – or Her. The desire of man is turned towards her, towards them as a source of life and wisdom. From her, from them, he receives a truth that suits his need for soul: an earth in which it will be possible for new words to germinate, provided that faith, trust, attraction are cultivated. A passion without faithfulness to her, to them, too immediate in its inclination, does not leave a place for the soul and its becoming. Nor does a turning away from or a forgetting of her, of them. The measure for an appropriate relation to her, to them – and Her – has to be discovered. Words and gestures need to be invented – saying the divine that compels man to pursue his becoming.

There, man has lost his way. He has not cultivated the inclination for her, for them – and Her. He has closed this path between earth and the heavens. In order to not acknowledge his error, he has labeled as temptation his penchant for her, for them. Only those who were useful for constructing his world survived: the guardians of the hearth or the city, the mothers of men or of gods. Those, thus, who submitted to his desire, without exchanges or dialogues with them – men remaining between themselves. The daughter also retains an interest for man, that of a good to be left, for compensation, to other men. Only with men does communication exist, but it amounts to a commercial exchange of goods, including cultural goods, and not to a dialogue between persons.

The first occurrence of this dialogue, its advent in part still and always to come, takes place between him and her. But it does not exist without distance, and even non-Being, between the two. Something that appears intolerable to the new wisdom of man. He wants what is full, closed, created by him. And he confuses what is with his own necessities. He does not understand that, through this doing, he interrupts the becoming of the living, and dries up the source of his desire. Becoming attached to this or that thing, to this or that task, this or that word, his impetus becomes fixed, stops, thus broken up.

The hypothesis of a beyond regarding things and words, of a Being or void or ultimate hole to be respected, ensures a dynamic revival of the will. But this revival is of a different nature: more abstract and constrained than that surge which carried him towards her, towards them, with enthusiasm and trust. Now he endeavours to do everything, all by himself, thanks to the teaching received from a master. He no longer likes to turn, to return, towards her – or Her. He refuses generation, including that of desire. He wants to make, construct, fabricate the world, his world – denying, disowning his provenance from her, from them. He will leave there only a kind of in-draft, opening towards the unlimited of the before and the after for which he no longer wishes in the present.

Multiple, she is also one

Her, he can neither seize nor grasp. He cannot transform her into a thing, or into a word. Too multiple, mobile, fluid, she escapes his control, exceeds his categories. And, when he believes he has reached her, penetrated her, she is no longer there, nothing anymore – vanished, elsewhere, otherwise. It is impossible to say that she simply is, but also that she is not, at least if she is considered in herself. She is, but not solid, nor uniform, nor finite. She is, but also void, multiple, indefinite. Infinite? She resists the limits that he intends to impose on her, including his strategy of the opposites presumed to transpose the real into a world that he dominates, confusing in this the movement of growth with a change of degree in a world based on quantity. She brings together within herself the opposites: both mother of god(s) and whore, for example. But the poles between which he tears her apart frustrate his own attraction, and interrupt her becoming. It is no longer her – or Her – that he desires but representations that he has forged to enclose her in his world. He retains of her only ideas or images peculiar to himself, and the one he encloses in his house, in his world, in his name or names, is no longer her. Even if she accepts to dwell there. Through innocence, fear, forgetting or ignorance concerning her path – what she is, what she can become.

She is also led out of her way because of the disappearance of Her, the one whom he did not reveal to her. Concealing from her what she can transmit to him, inspire in him. Another sowing of his inner land, of his soul, of which he is unaware for lack of having recognized it, cultivated it, and having respected what was irreducible to himself in it in order to ensure its existence, its growth. Some seeds die when one wants to assimilate them, to make them one's own, instead of offering them a hospitable place to take root, to develop, to blossom.

Has it not been so for the birth of speech, which can take place only between two different human beings? Only there does speech assume its meaning as an exchange of truths, of wisdoms between two irreducible to one – or One – two irreducible to the same. And, in this way, it brings to the attraction the relief or support that it needs in order to remain and to develop as desire.

Speech, then, says the person as such in the relation to the other. It does not stop at naming what is external to this person, the objects or things that surround him, or her; it does not represent an instrument of more or less conscious mastery of the reality of the world. It makes a mental, affective, corporeal state transmissible, one aroused by the other in particular. It speaks (of) the self but also (of) the other in the self. It elaborates the possibility of a bond between the two. It permits to defer the immediacy of the attraction, it works towards its transposition into a shareable desire. Compelling me to take the time to experience, to think, to express, it also offers to the other a time to listen, to acknowledge – the other, the self – a time to find a response appropriate to the present situation. The imperatives of instinct, of need, whether real or fictive, are then thwarted and entry into the properly human world of desire is laid out little by little. With this world a culture of dialogue between two different human beings is worked out, the most fundamental site for the construction of the human as such.

There the most ambiguous term is not the best. The word that favours the duality of persons is preferable, and not the one that claims to hold the key to diverse possible meanings. The many-faceted word or formula evokes a power that man borrows from the divine: in order to prophesize or to cure. This word is a talisman, an enigma, a thing, and not a word for communicating with the other, for transmitting something of oneself in order to develop the relation with him, or her. It is a word through which the miracle worker conceals rather than unveils. Then the relation with the other is no longer privileged in its possible, even asymmetrical, reciprocity. Meaning is no longer given, no longer exchanged. It is trapped or paralyzed in an enigma to which no precise signification corresponds. The value of the word is reversed. Made in order to pass on, to disclose or reveal, it becomes what breaks off communication, exchange, sharing: what masks and hides. A fetish-symbol of the power of a master, a school, a church or a society, it aims above all to fascinate, to subjugate.

This word conveys again, without saying so, a mystery that concerns her – or Her. A mystery that exceeds him, but that he perceived, at least partially, in the meeting with Her. He is his guardian without being able to decipher or express it. The mystery will be conveyed as an enigma through a discourse that is not addressed to her, but instead is made to forget her. Through a message spoken to other men, and first to disciples, in which, without being told, a divine of unknown origin will be held. Armed with this enigma, man confronts the gods of his gender, defying them with his skill in creating a world, in handling words, in playing with a meaning that he himself does not know. He thus tries to enclose it with some container and to retain it through this stratagem. At least as long as he remembers it, as long as the inexpressible of the flesh is not dissipated into artifices, pretenses, calculations, but also into more or less magical rituals, gestures and words. All that remains is the form or the formula; the real content that they were supposed to contain, to safeguard, has escaped from them.

By wanting to appropriate what he has received from her – or Her – man has been deprived of it, has lost it. To recall it would imply that he remembers her – or Her – including in himself. And that he looks for a way to adress her, to them, and express what he perceived. Praise, a neither abstract nor ritual praise, no doubt would have safeguarded the presence of her, of them – outside of him and in him. Stammering perhaps, but not repetitive. A celebration attempting to say her in her concrete multitude, but not contradictory for all that. So is she cool but also warm, depending on the place and the moment – in her own becoming and in approaching her. If she were only cold and damp, she would simply repulse, except perhaps there where the dry longs for a source. If she were only fire, she would burn away and no one could find presence or dwelling in her. Rather she unites contrasts, of which she assures the living metabolism, in turn passionate awakening of the lover and return to virginity. Without the one, she would not know the other, at least in a permanent way. These states are not for all that opposed or mutually exclusive. They support one another in their blossoming and their becoming – the best lover being the one who is still and always virgin. A virginity tied to a capacity for being faithful to the self, an aptitude for remaining in oneself, regardless of any specular or speculative narcissism. This place of permanence of the self in oneself and with oneself, a more fresh and lofty place, allows the fire of attraction to ascend and to become love, listening, speech, thought. Without it, desire does not last, and has difficulty in being said to the other.

If the cold and the hot, the damp and the dry are in her, she also participates in becoming and permanence, mobility and immobility. For herself, but not only for herself. Indeed, she engenders attraction, movement towards, but also the child. She is fecund of what she produces in the other, fecund also of the other. Which is not without effect on her – who flowers or bears fruit depending on the moment and comes out changed, in appearance but also in her material or spiritual nature. She produces – in her, outside of her, in herself. Unlike man who contents himself with the same in his productions, remaining amongst the same ones as himself notably in and for his exchanges, she engenders the different as well as the same. And it is more with the different that she enjoys exchanging. Even being exchanged, not like a thing and for some other thing or some money, but in herself. The virgin daughter changing into a lover or a spouse, into the mother of the child or companion. Into sister also, and friend. Assisting becoming – of the other, of the world. Compassionate, almost by nature. On the condition that she return to herself, be faithful to herself – be still and always virgin. Provided this is understood as being able to overcome dependence, to become and remain a woman. Autonomous, free, listening to what she is, to whom she is. Otherwise, devouring, envious, demanding, harassing. Always begging for what no one can grant to her: herself. If not, sovereign – multiply, indefinitely. Infinitely, if this is not understood as an extension without limits. This infinite instead evokes an experience that at the very instant corresponds perfectly to aspiration, or to taste.

Indeed, she is not without sensible qualities. In this sense, whoever knows her or recognizes her does not fear the abyss. She accompanies the becoming with a support of the senses that is not a spiritual diversion but an homage to life. To celebrate this is in no way a misdeed but rather a prayer – awakening eyes, ears, taste, smell, touch to a function other than that of ensuring survival, appropriation, consumption. Perceptions become paths of the soul, paths towards the soul. They open and unfold the soul without taking it away from its respiration, its breath, its invisibly tactile origin. They light up our life, transfigure it, transubstantiate it while preserving it as life. They transform it into humanity, enriching it with a new existence.

The living, from then on, assumes another appearance. Far from mystery becoming an enigma in which truth is forgotten, far from the mask or the fetish becoming the façade or container of any power, the transmutation of the living makes it appear differently in her, through her – no longer a separation between the secret and what would veil it, but an irradiation of the invisible through a visible covering. She gives herself to be seen otherwise, but this radiance is in a way the inverse of a divine hidden under some masquerade. It offers to eyes a spectacle that transcends the vision of a body. The transfiguration is given to be seen; it transports the one who perceives it. Bringing us face to face with a mystery and not into subjection to a power, except the one that man himself will fabricate instead of contemplating and accepting the transmitted teaching without simply appropriating it. Searching for the way of its respect, of its commemoration, without making it his own.

To celebrate such an event, to cultivate its remembrance, does not amount to capturing it, to possessing it. Something man has often done: striving to repeat or mimic the effect produced on himself, while being mistaken about its origin. Searching for, even creating, magic where there was a spiritual transformation of matter. Inventing more or less esoteric cults and rituals, objects or things more or less comparable to fetishes or idols, ambiguous or enigmatic words in order to delimit what eludes him, what flees before his attempt to seize it.

Praise for the gift received, the quest for gestures or words to render thanks, the conversion of oneself to welcome more fittingly the one who is unsparing of it were more suitable for celebrating and commemorating the event. It was necessary, in order to succeed in this, to accept that the difference between her and him exists and that it is a source of benefits to be respected without claiming to appropriate them.

Something then happens that does not oppose saying to being seen, the word to the idol, but that transforms the one and the other. Words are modified in order to be appropriate for praise and the body is transfigured, in part through this change of discourse. This becoming is possible thanks to respect for the difference between her and him. It first takes place in an acknowledgement of her, or Her, by him and a search for gestures or words in order to celebrate what she gives, on this side of or beyond any object or thing – what she transmits to him, which he does not perceive clearly or misjudges. Imagining from then on himself to be a god, filled with so many treasures, or sending back the origin and the gift of breath, of soul, of the word into God. Considering himself to be the 'all knowing,' and the 'all saying' to an ignorant and deficient disciple. Never having become man. This can only occur in the relation with her, and the recognition of what, in him, comes from her – a gift that should inspire speech.

Man does not become man all by himself. And to appeal to the gods, or to a God, does not suffice for the accomplishment of such a task. The relation with the other part of humanity – mother, lover, daughter, goddess – is essential.

Neither animal nor god, but not yet man

The language that man forges in order to appeal to the god(s), in order to designate his surroundings or exchange information with his peers does not yet suit a speech of man as man. It corresponds, perhaps, to that of an evolved species, capable of appropriating objects, things, the world from a distance and of storing them differently in his memory. The linguistic tool of the human would perhaps be more efficient than that of another species for dominating the real and transforming it. Yet would this be, for all that, a task specific to humanity as such? In an initial phase of its constitution? A conquering but still defensive phase? In which it is a question of differentiating himself from other species in order to ensure his survival? Is that already to exist as humanity? Or to prepare a place in order to be able, one day, to reach it?

The function that language has fulfilled during this period would thus merit being put into perspective. Useful for survival and the elaboration of a framework making possible the appearance of a new species, language would not have displayed, or not yet discovered, in this way its properly human characteristics. Even in its calls to a leader, master or God, it would not be radically different from that of animal signs recognizing the leader of the herd or the queen of the hive. To be sure, if this God is supposed to refer to a real that goes beyond a present corporeal reality, he preserves a place for a future yet to come. In this reserve, the existence of the other as other can then be revealed. God or the gods – in the unity or the multiplicity of a super-human – would safeguard the possibility of a relation to the other. Unless he, or they, have captured and paralyzed it in a power of the same, or Same, postponed to infinite. The two eventualities are part of the ambiguity of a divine defined prior to the becoming of human being as man – and woman – and not as a still little differentiated neuter individual.

Such a divinity divides man into two parts, human and divine, called natural and supernatural. Instead of man learning to transform, to transfigure what he is from birth, he is led to consider that part of him as inferior and to neglect it for a becoming other than human. He thus disowns his being engendered by her and fails to cultivate this gift, either as such or as relation to her. He claims to have been created by a master or a God of his gender: origin and end of his journey. Then he hypostasizes his becoming both as source and as end. Abandoning responsibility for what he is to an Other formed in his own image – thus the Same. In this way exiled in a life of which he has not recognized the value, the truth. Always below or above what is possible for him at the moment. Climbing too high, falling too low – blind to what surrounds him as living.

Instead of becoming what he is, man has wanted to become what he is not. Leaping from animality to divinity, he has not cultivated his humanity. Of which reality and value cannot appear to him in the denial of her – or Her – in the ignorance that he represents only one part of humanity, and that humanity can be cultivated only by two, and in the respect for differences between the two parts. It is thus not all by himself that man can elaborate a speech. It is not all by himself that he can impose gods upon humanity or define the laws of the city, abolishing, through these laws, the value of the singularity and of difference. Men would have to agree on something common: a somehow invariable order imposing on all its relative abstraction, indeed its rigidity. What each one perceives of the world, of oneself, of the other is henceforth considered secondary, flimsy.

Then, the truth of what perception teaches must fade away in the face of that imposed by the common. One must renounce oneself in order to obey the law of the collective, and of the logos. With the hope, occasionally, of rising again by attaining the perception of a divine presence.

In this hope, also imposed, the difference fades between the resurrection granted to man in the context of the cults of Demeter thanks to fidelity to the Goddess and that thought to happen through faith in a God imperceptible in the present. The same words sometimes designate very diverse truths. Imperceptibly, man passes from the ones to the others, leaving himself in the present, also becoming extraneous to the current relation to the other. Prophecy prevails over speaking in the present, over dialogue. Speech becomes prediction or commemoration. It forgets its original function, the exchange with the other, through listening to the singularity of each one and uttering a proper truth. In the place of the 'hole' or the opaqueness of a birth, an interlacing of discourses is woven from which the human as such is engendered, and not only the substratum of its becoming. From then on the human participates in this becoming in the present and does not abandon it to some parental past, some divine future or some medical assistance – three substitutes for his task preventing him from fully accomplishing his humanity.

And the question of knowing whether the god reveals himself through the soothsayer, the warrior, the teacher or the bard neglects the fact that the divine work should first take place between man and woman. In this work, desire is not reduced to an ornament but represents the way itself, in which man does not advance alone but with the other – each part of humanity embodying the divine for, thanks to, and with its second part.

Outside of this properly human task there are only illusion, vainglory. And immoderation grows. Besides the fact that seeing is henceforth opposed to hearing, even though both are required in a relation of truth with the other here present. A truth that does not exclude a portion of invisibility, of mystery that, sometimes, transfigures seeing itself – inspiring speech, without paralyzing listening. If the thing seen saturates the pupil, does the saying of it not become useless? But if something invisible remains, what is seen does not exclude a speech accompanying it. Then words will no longer necessarily aim to designate or name what has appeared. They will wish, above all, to celebrate this appearing as such, or address to it a testimony of what awakens in the one who looks at it.

From then on, the senses can be joined together. Seeing no longer excludes hearing. And their union requires inventing a new speech, more consonant with the relation between two humans – the seizure through a name continually risking subjecting the one to the other or the two to a third. This speech opens a space for dialogue in which the one does not look while the other listens. In which mystery is not referred to God, and woman is not reduced to a nature without soul, or speech. In which the human and the divine are present in the exchange of looks and words between woman and man, women and men.

This stage of human becoming is still lacking. The first speaker had contemplated the Goddess; he probably failed to listen to her and did not speak to her. It is somewhere else that he will accomplish such gestures. He will address himself to the disciple in order to teach him how to designate the world. He will compel him to listen, on pain of being excluded from the city. He will otherwise force woman to listen, no doubt. As for him, he will listen to his peers for what is already said, and will consult the god for what is still to be said. He will hear from men what is already named, what is repeated and, from some god, what would still be unknown, still to come. The original hole into which the Goddess has disappeared is filled with the material of words, sealed by the logos, opening towards a future in which it is the god who speaks, invisible.

She is at the source of the saying, the one that, perhaps, he saw but to whom he did not speak. In the end, he substitutes for her god(s) of his own gender from whom he awaits a revelation, which he both wants and does not want.

Since there is no evocation of her, of the one from whom it has its source, the soul seems without limits inasmuch as his logos is profound – the soul that he has appropriated, that he has adapted to himself, making it his creation. A soul and a logos, which can grow or diminish without the intervention of her, the one who conceived. A soul that would henceforth find its origin in the authorized words of the master, in which the forgetting of her – or Her – is overshadowed. A soul whose energy is supposed to ascend towards the god or descend towards servitude in accordance with the logos on which it is founded. Whatever the case, it is cut off from life, from vigor, from blood, from breath – at least the original ones. Energy whose movement is already secondary in relation to the living, whereas it could have been its flowering. Provided that one is faithful – to self, to the other, to difference.

From then on, a bad infinite founded upon an artificial growth is imposed as a horizon. That which is common to all will arrest this opening. But the common amounts neither to the living nor to the true. Speech, unanchored from its origin, searches for weight in rhetoric or logic, which become sophistic strategies if they no longer obey the economy of life, of breath, of the relation in difference – between him and her, or Her.

Some are not content with a forced apnea. They want to retrace their steps, or wait for the god at the crossroads. And even entrust their nose with the secret of the reality of things, thus what still remembers the air, the passage of the breath between outside and inside, inside and outside. That nose thanks to which man begins to exist without her. Not yet seeing forms, but already perceiving differences through smell: that between others and one's mother, that between men and the gods. It would not only be a name but a fragrance that would identify the god. The one who exists on this side of or beyond all opposites, who nullifies them by assembling them.

Inspiration is sometimes a more reliable path than the logos for recognizing the truth. However, it remains the gesture of a living being, and the god claims to be immortal, beyond life. The logos will lead towards him, a logos that mimics the living but does not know death. Exiled from sensory, and even emotional, experiences, man tries to find it again through excess – exploits, heroism, fame.

The sage then rebels against passion: he searches for himself in withdrawal, reflection, self-knowledge. The injunction 'Know thyself' is prepared, as is the taste of the philosopher for death. In order to get over this austere, even depressing, confrontation, he frequents his peers, plays at learning to reason, devotes himself to logical and rhetorical debates. He distracts his attention from life that no longer becomes. The relation to her, to nature or woman, and to their divinity, is lacking.

Thus deprived of enthusiasm, of attraction, of freshness, mental energy falls off, grows dulled, dreams of appearances of the real. Too tense, too hot, too saturated, man finds relief with young boys, letting his seed, be it logical or otherwise, flow into them. And a new life springs from it, which will survive death. This proof of the immortality of his seed consoles man. He forgets that it already is immortal by nature – as is, moreover, the seed of the woman. Some of their genes, their sexual chromosomes, overcome death and are incarnated in descendants to whom they impart certain features.

Why has man appropriated this privilege? Why has he likened the woman's part in generation to a simple nourishing environment, keeping for himself providing for the germ of individuation? And how does it happen that this error has remained ignored for so long? Its consequences for the conception and birth of the truth are decisive. Truth can be engendered only by the two genders. A thing that a tradition has tried to neglect, to deny, to forget.

And yet a child inherits forms and other features from its mother as well as from its father. The contribution of the mother is not limited to that of nourishment in order that the features that the father would have supplied with his seed can develop. The participation of woman in engendering is as much genetic as it is somatic. If this were not the case, a human genealogy would be impossible, except by means of cloning and a reproduction of replicas. Which does not amount to engendering.

How, for centuries, could such ignorance, such blindness survive? They have brought about a proliferation of replicas and artifices progressively growing away from life and from human being itself. A culture in the masculine has mimicked life, just as a man is mimicked through cloning. Neither the logos nor an only masculine God have really transcended the natural world. They have artificially replicated it for lack of having found how to express a movement of natural growth. To succeed in reproducing all alone, man has had to interrupt the continuity of the becoming of life, cutting it off from its roots. A form would then be presumed to be able to serve as a model for the proliferation of replicas confused with the true.

4

The wandering of man

A becoming cut off from its carnal source

Becoming can take form(s) thanks to an engendering by two different beings. It is not necessary, for man, to cut himself off from life in order that forms might exist, but to couple his life with that of the other, woman, in order to engender forms going from the most natural to the most spiritual of their incarnation. Man and woman can engender together bodies as well as culture, a culture which will then better conform to physiological necessities, to affects, to speech, to ideas. Although it can fulfill a different function depending on the level to which it corresponds, form always exists. It is thanks to form(s) that man and woman exchange, communicate, whether the form(s) appear(s) as object, gesture, figure, image, rule, language, etc. or simple sensible experience. Everything assumes a form – more or less physical, more or less stable, more or less fluid, more or less vague, more or less visible….. In this form two subjectivities unite with one another, express or symbolize themselves in a manner that is more or less material or immaterial, more or less momentary or lasting, speaking more or less to one or another sense.

Instead of promoting forms conceived by two different subjectivities, the logos has been constituted starting from forms conceived by one alone, one who has, furthermore, all alone ensured their linking together. In order that they last, such forms need to be mental, kinds of representations coded by man, whose memory will be guaranteed in a cryptographic way. Only those who belong to certain societies – of men – can communicate with this language. Its rather abstract, arbitrary, artificial encoding makes it accessible to many provided that its usage, if not its sense, has been learned from a master. It is he who decides on the relevance of the coding. And whoever objects that he does not perceive the world in the same way will be declared incompetent, excluded from gatherings, labeled as backward or mad.

The master worked out the logos starting from his perception of the world, at least in the beginning. What is obscured of the life of her – or Her – in this perception will be doomed to be forgotten. Indeed if the logos, in the beginning, alludes to that, it does not bear witness, or barely does so, to the fact it is engendered by two: she, or She, being the one who at first transmits. This presence of her – or Her – is erased, in the coded representation, by passing to the timeless and insensible level of the idea. Once such a separation is made, any present manifestation will henceforth be assessed according to a model.

The master claims to hold the source of the truth, and he fixes it in Ideas, the only forms intelligible for him, in relation to which he will measure every other approach to the real as imperfect.

Man does not have, or no longer has, an understanding about the sensible, nor even about the natural – these realities elude him. He needs constructed frameworks thanks to which he can obtain some representation of them. In their very life, they hide from him. He describes them as secondary, because of powerlessness or vexation, and for lack of having cultivated them in the relation with her, or Her. For lack of having remained faithful to listening to nature, to the Goddess, and of having tried to dialogue with his other human, woman.

From then on, language is no more than a means to univocally appropriate things, to dominate them from on high starting from an idea that man gets of them. The universe is already coded, as it will be by scientific formulas attempting to define its properties and to act upon them. The universe is more and more coded rather than said by the logos. And men express among themselves their will to master and not what they are in their wholeness, in particular not what they are for one another, by one another.

Men speak and speak to one another starting from a universe, cut into words and concatenations of words, parallel to the living world from which the logos divides more and more. They communicate by repeating, not by saying what is present here and now – of the world, of themselves. Hence comes a combination of self-importance, drowsiness, and anger. Men are no longer there where their discourse places them. Between what they say and what they live, more or less fully, a part of them wanders. A part that hopes for its talents, for luck, for the gods, and that rebels against its powerlessness, gets worked up because of an energy that remains uncultivated. In order that gatherings or communities not be troubled, the dualism of body-soul, or better body-spirit, becomes more and more essential. The part of man, of men, which expresses emotions, uncontrollable by the logos, will be excluded from the city, or at best sent back home. Where man would have had possibilities of finding a new awakening, another path, a culture less distanced from the real, if speaking did not imply an arbitrary mastery of nature of which women and children, excluded from such an education, were not capable. What submission to the common discourse of between-men will have provoked as a disturbance of energy will become blind instinctual violence towards woman, authoritarianism of the head of the family over children, and first of all over the spouse. All of these are presumed to belong to the world of nature – henceforth parallel to the logos – that man intends to dominate.

Men no longer want to believe in her – nor in Her. They mean to grow by themselves, and appropriate the world without her, without them. Appropriating the world in an instant and all at once is impossible. Men, thus, cut it into pieces and try to put it back together again in a suitable manner. As the pieces are no longer animated with her life, nor with a life of their own, men must create a dynamic to assemble these pieces into a whole. They create it through opposition, conflict, even hatred, over which rules an indifference that claims to arbitrate in a neutral way.

Not being inspired by her speaking, no longer naming Her as the source of saying, man wanders – sometimes conscious of a gap or a hole in his horizon, possibly covered by the One, sometimes worrying about the emptiness of his words, his actions, even his perceptions, at best sensing in everything both her presence and her absence, and speaking of Being to which everything belongs, including himself.

From this Being he uproots himself through words that are only denominations, words of man who wanders and also cause to wander while providing beacons for this wandering. Words in search of their truth at best in conversations between friends or from environing things. A truth of an exile, never confident of his roots, trying to open a path among conflicts between two opposites rather than in faithfulness to his origin. This origin has been lost, forgotten. It is absent from the words pronounced, exchanged with peers. Their meaning serves more to regulate a survival than to support a growth proper to life.

Such growth cannot happen outside of a faithfulness to her – or Her – the one who gives life, who inspires or maintains love, she whom one knows without knowing her, through a knowledge irreducible to the logic of opposites. The one who stays outside of every exclusive predicate. Being neither this nor that, she is. At the source of every perception, truth, meaningful word, she cannot amount to any of these. She is – elusive, unpredicable, unsayable. However, she is more present than all that can be seized, predicated, said. She sometimes reveals herself in a contemplative silence, a love without object, a letting be that man no longer knows, that he has forgotten by forgetting the one who has passed on or granted life to him – a life that she has let be and grow in her. He substitutes for her a void, a hole, a neuter 'there is' or 'it is,' the One of a construction parallel to the life from which Being would arise, or even a God who would have created him. He then closes the horizon without her – or Her – she who has kept her world open for him. A gesture alien to his universe, a sharing that is unknown to him, that he does not succeed in evaluating, thinking, saying. That he can, at the very most, sometimes sing, by transposing her into some figure or allegory, more or less divine, which is already no longer at the source of life. Such a representation is already too defined, encircled with forms, surrounded by borders, even when she is goddess of the infinite – of love, which always goes beyond the proper horizon. A love which, due to lack of limits, risks annihilating the one, the other, the link between the two. For lack of accepting to let be, without wanting to capture, to master – first of all life, which she grants with love. The one does not go without the other.

This incapacity or this refusal to let be has modified the relation of man to the other, and to the world. Instead of contemplating them, singing them, opening himself to them and giving thanks for all they offer, man has withdrawn into himself to master what may reach him from the outside, to dominate it or appropriate it. He provides himself with a soul that was no longer made of breath relating to the whole of the living world, that it could celebrate, praise with gestures, but also with words. A soul of the universe with which the soul of man could communicate, commune, as it could be with the soul of the other, including the different other. Including the woman and the mother, who, as living beings, have a relation to breath and, as engenderers, have a privileged and spiritual relation to air, which they give from the beginning to the fetus, through their blood, for its life, its growth.

He provided himself with a soul, a sort of self-consciousness, which was no longer a hymn to life for the surplus that it lavished on him, but was instead a logical creation that established a world parallel to life, and whose growth always risks going either well or poorly, is always dangerous, because it is unfaithful to a natural origin. Hence the wandering, including the spiritual wandering, of Western man. Hence also the multiple conflicts, often murderous, if not of body at least of the heart or soul, in the name of what would be the right way, or of the one who would hold the only truth, the only knowledge that matters. These conflicts already take place within man himself between his natural belonging and a spiritual becoming that claims to master it, to govern it.

Failing to respect the two of gender that is necessary for the existence and becoming of humanity, man got split into two, becoming body and soul. He got divided, in himself, between the earthly and the heavenly. The one and the other have been deprived of their living, real enrootedness. The one and the other began to wander in search of a possible survival thanks to an existence constructed in a more or less artificial way. The one and the other became orphans – and from themselves. And they quested for possible re-creators of their origin, their unity – the master, the doctor, the logician, the moralist. Soon the priest? The politician? All strove to provide a natural belonging, cut off from itself, with clothing that suits it, adjusts it according to acceptable common norms – norms decreed to be human, and that suppose a self-mastery capable of adhering to a model of humanity. Something, someone is absent from its definition: the natural origin, and she who gives it. The two are contained, repressed, forgotten in man, and soon extrapolated into some divinity capable of accounting for them. A creator God?

Torn apart, man projects himself onto the beyond

Excluding her – or Her – from his becoming, and even from his origin, has led man to a schism in the unity of the self. If some who still believe in her – or Her – experience wandering and exile, oscillating between adversity and completeness, hatred and love, unless they search for a substitute for her starting from which to form their being or Being, others replace the two of the duality of genders with the dualism body–soul, or earthly–heavenly, a prelude to all the other sorts of dichotomies. Man can come to terms with himself alone, without her, only by dividing himself. And even his way of taking care of himself becomes dual: gymnastics of the body or exercises of the spirit.

What the relation to the other could bring as a possibility for a progressive evolution of each individual faithful to a/his proper unity no longer exists. The passage from elementary vitality to a culture of breath, of love, of thought with a view towards a human becoming and coexistence is lost.

As seems to be lost the power to cure that breath, love, thought once had. Thus begins the era of doctors of the body likely to care for certain ills thanks to appropriate techniques.

At the same time as her – or Her – disappears a certain relation to the god(s). As if they were, in a more or less mysterious way, linked to her existence, and to the relation between him and her. Man is left on his own split between nature and an all-powerful divinity, which he created in his own image, according to a dream of completeness and situated in the beyond. He then definitively establishes the scission between natural and spiritual, nature and culture. Torn between the two, wandering between the two, in search of a master of his own gender able to guide him.

Imperceptibly, his soul made of respiration, of breath, of a surplus of life, his soul, an heir of her – and Her – becomes the result of using a logos inherited from the master, assumed to ensure a survival after death. Man has not little by little transformed his natural belonging into a spiritual identity, he has situated the former on this side and the latter on the other side of his present existence. An existence in which he is in quest of himself through wandering, metamorphosis, evolution towards a human status founded more on death than on life. Captured in forms, words, celestial figures, life freezes in the expectation of a better beyond. Life, breath, love, thought are hanging onto a potential future, the result of a becoming that man has not – not yet? – succeeded in working out with her, or Her.

From then on divided in himself, man projects this scission onto the exterior world – where differences exist, to be sure, and contrasts, but not real oppositions. There is a contrast between night and day, winter and springtime, for example. Yet they are not for all that in opposition, unless man projects onto them his own inner conflicts, or wants to master them by removing the transitions between them. Now these transitions belong to a rhythm of life which cannot be mastered, except through a caricature that transforms the one and the other into opposites. They are then only images, words, functions deprived of life. And the same will happen to man and woman, no longer considered as living beings who are different but as opposite representations, names, functions or roles.

For lack of solving the question of his origin thanks to an appropriate relation with her – and Her – man experiences life as a drama, torn between opposites, blind to his destiny. Instead of advancing step by step towards a more human becoming – at once corporeal and spiritual – he is split into body and soul, shared out between the two of whom he is born, by whom he has been engendered and who, in him, ought in a sense to become one. Not having, thus, to forsake the one for the other, but to discover little by little the mystery of their union.

This requires man to remember the breathing received from the mother, thanks to which the fetus, and even more the newborn, gain their first autonomy, the germ of a soul. A culture of breathing, the transformation of a respiration of survival into a spiritual breath, is necessary for the development of man towards humanity. And it is a culture of love and of thought that can animate the breath, including with fire. The opposition between breath and fire can solely be a source of drama, and lead progressively to death. This tragedy is so radical that it ends not only in dividing man himself and the world that surrounds him, but also the gods. Henceforth, they will be creators or destroyers, unifying or dividing, loving or hating. Such oppositions are attributed even to Her, the goddess of love, sometimes called Aphrodite and sometimes Neikos.

Because he did not cultivate his relation with the one who is at the origin of life, with the one who brought him into the world and directed him towards autonomy, man not only splits into body and soul but projects onto her – and Her – a source of life and death.

And this separation between good and bad, lucky and unlucky, substituting for a gradual becoming of oneself, spreads over everything, and pollutes the human and divine environment which man needs as a dwelling place, in some way placental, while waiting for gaining a complete autonomy – thanks in particular to a cultivation of the relation with her, and Her. Which has not yet happened. Greek man is still joined with his natural environment, to which he is open, from which he receives benefits for his existence, which fills him with wonder and which he sings. But, little by little, he divides from it to win a supposedly autonomous soul, a soul that is no longer the house of god, at least of an unambiguous god. This god has already been substituted for her – and Her – transforming life, breath, fire into works that are more or less good.

The god has become an enigma hiding the mystery of her – and Her. The mystery of life and of the difference that inhabits and animates it – for its growth, its flowering, its reproduction. A mystery that is sensed, respected, venerated, sung, but never mastered. Man can distance himself from it, even forget it, yet the mystery remains and calls to him – be this only through the threat of a planetary destruction, of the loss of his power, in particular of his power to fecundate.

In the beginning it is his own splitting up, his dispersal and that of the world which surrounds him that bear witness to a non-respect for the mystery of the other that can give man, and even god, a unity. For lack of bowing before this inappropriable mystery, of resorting to silence, to the song of praise and the poetic language that can express something of it, man enters into a fractured, ambiguous world, a noisy world, in which everything is at once equivalent and opposed, in which one searches for the way by passing from one opposite to the other, by reversing them in one another. And by trying to bring them together or to merge them in the One, the Whole – the God. A God who closes the horizon of becoming, organizing it according to a constructed end and not from a received natural origin.

The God, from then on, confers unity, gives meaning, prescribes the path. Extrapolating in this way the real, natural difference of life into the Absolute, the Infinite, making all other differences relative, and substitutable in relation to it, indeed transforming these differences into conflictual oppositions in which the strongest wins. War is substituted for a respect for the mystery – for the other. The right question henceforth is that of finding the appropriate weapon in order to conquer – and language, the logos, little by little becomes the sovereign weapon between the same ones. Who will discover the words and their combination likely to bring victory? War changes location, leaving the battlefield, it overruns the court. It also moves from the body to the soul.

A multiplicity of signs – whose organization more or less expresses meaning, moreover a more or less valid and exhaustive meaning – is substituted for the multiplicity of the living, which does not deprive each one of his or her own vitality and growth. It is no longer a question of only naming the god appropriate to this or that dimension or aspect of human existence, but of producing the meaning by oneself, a meaning more and more ultimate and unifying – to which a God will little by little correspond, a God for whom no particular name is still suitable, who no longer really has a name. He is presumed to gather all the names together starting from a beyond out of man's reach, at least during his earthly life – before this God comes to pass, the One unifying the whole. Alone, holding himself apart from all, outside of every dualistic organization, this God still perhaps evokes the trace of her, or Her. Thus a mysterious memory, extraneous to any designation, from which the sage, in his solitude, could not escape. A memory into which he is or has been merged, instead of the stakes, without image or name, of his contemplation having been perpetuated. That which still mysteriously gave meaning to his words has been forgotten. In its place, a certain emptiness, a certain distress occur, the beginning of a wandering and of annoyances or conflicts concerning the way to be followed.

The One of the God is not the One of the Wise Thing. The latter cannot, at least in the beginning, be designated with the name of a god, not even that of the God of gods: Zeus. She is irreducible to god – or God – at least at that time. And thus some seek to appropriate her through the unity that the logos tries to form. They are hostile to whatever remembers two – genders, generations, truths, ways, etc. What matters is to create, to recreate from some One, beyond the multiple into which she has been divided, that she has become, for lack of having been recognized as one – her. In order not to endlessly disintegrate himself, man needs a guarantee for his unity other than that of his own nature. He searches for it through an agreement with the same ones as himself, forged by means of an instrument constituting a new whole, parallel to that of nature: the logos. Henceforth, only the company of the one who has re-created himself by using the logos seems a human partnership to him. Men construct a world of their own on a forgetting, and even a contempt, of her. It would not be wise to remember what she represents for them – an inaccessible thing that it is advisable to renounce.

But that does not happen without difficulty: dereliction, an ambivalence in feelings, an absence of horizon, a both horizontal and vertical splitting up of the world. On pain of perishing – like an animal, a slave, and even a man or a god – man must give himself back a One. Everything will then receive another meaning.

The One cannot stay only in the place of his natural origin. That would escape his mastery. Moreover, strictly speaking, his natural origin does not correspond only to one – or One – but to two, something that remains imperceptible, invisible to him. Instead of recognizing the attributes of every one contributing to his natural engendering, and trying to find how to cultivate the relation with each of these, he stands between she whom he in some way puts under his feet and he whom he situates little by little in the beyond of an extraterrestrial heaven. The weaving that he should have carried out in himself between her and him, between mother and father, is missing. Lost, he wanders between opposites which speak of an absence of continuity between his natural origin and the unity for which he searches. In order to avoid a constant laceration and uncertainty, he strives to remove the opposition in the same, to bring the opposites together in the one – or the One – able to combine all the attributes, as opposed as they may be.

Step by step, he thus makes his way towards some god – or God – in the masculine. A god – or God – who unites all the opposites, holds all of them, and who each at first names according to his taste. A god who would establish the link between the two poles of himself? With this done, some God, yet unnamed, is substituted for her – and Her – without any alliance between her or Her and him or Him having occurred. There where she – or She – was, he – or He – is. Or rather would be.

Because he – or He – yet is starting from a construction and a faith that do not take into account the whole of being. He is starting from a doing and a saying that sometimes go well and sometimes go badly, sorts of attempts to recreate thanks to which he tries to give himself an autonomous existence in relation to her, to the surrounding world and to the god(s). This is achieved through the elaboration of an interiority resulting from the correct use of speech – of the logos. He tries to construct a linking of words that give him a soul of his own – in some way a beginning of subjectivity – capable of being and growing by itself, independently of her – and Her – and of the living world that surrounds him. He seeks how to manipulate words in order to put life and the gods in his service. How to choose the words? How to associate them? What attributes to retain among the contrasting experiences he has of the world in all its complexity? And how to join them all together, to combine them with one another? What Whole, what One is able to respect this? What being could collect all these attributes?

The sacred character of the master-disciple relation

Believing that he can succeed in dominating the world thanks to the new weapon he is forging, man does not see how this begins to enclose him in a sort of double of himself. The logos that he wanted to be the instrument of a neuter and universal wisdom develops little by little according to his own necessities, cutting him off from the rest of the world – and in particular from her, and Her. Pure nature or mere virgin according to his fantasies.

He has not recognized her in her particular unity, and her further ability to give life to another body, and even to another soul. This notion of unity remains extraneous to him. He is suspicious of it, moves away from it, and from all that maintains a link with her: life, breath, fluid. He wants to go beyond the coexistence, even the communion, between the living beings that he experienced with her, but not with the permanence that he wished. Wanting to take control at least of time, he searches for another solution more suitable to his measure, or immoderation. He abandons soul for spirit, breath for fire. Air – the element thanks to which he gained his first autonomy as a newborn, that is at the beginning and end of life, that can unify the body – is no longer considered as the decisive element in his anthropology and his cosmology. Fire supplants it, trying to organize and dominate water, on the one hand, and the earth, on the other. Henceforth, man and his environment are in an unstable balance. Rising up, but not without destroying life in this erection. In the name of the god?

Some perceive that worshiping the god lacks moderation. They attempt to substitute a wise and ordered discourse for rites, and a relation between men for the relation to the god. Substituting another human being for a mental representation or a statue was not without sense. But why another man and, preferably, a man of another generation? Why would the relation between those who are the same, a relation based on a transfer of wisdom between men, be more wise than a relation with the god? Because man has appropriated the part of god? And because he has transposed prayer from the temple to a conversation between men, and even more so to the relation of teaching between men? Does he not thus sacrifice, for a second time, the real of life to a mastery by discourse? In the beginning, a sharing respectful of life with her thanks to a soul made of breath was sacrificed to the privilege of fire reserved for the relation with the god. Then, the divine fire was domesticated in an ordered and methodical teaching between master and disciple. However understandable the longing of man to go beyond the reality of things may be, the question arises of knowing why the way of destruction, of sacrifice has been privileged and not that of a transformation of the real – of life, of desire, of love? What impatience and what thirst for mastery have determined such choices?

The development of the soul as a cultivation of breath, a reserve of life able to assume diverse temperatures, scents, colours has been replaced by a conception of the soul as fire. A fire that mixes with nothing but burns, consumes what it touches, leading at best towards a resurrection or a repro-duction. An unstable fire, which can awaken but not serve as medium, as mediator, at least not in its fiery immediacy. A fire that it is thus advisable to domesticate between humans, in fact between men – even disregarding its cultivation between man and god, not to speak of that between man and woman.

It is through conversations among wise men and, even more, through teaching between a wise man and an inexperienced adolescent that fire is cultivated. In order to escape orgiastic passion, it is neutralized by a saying. But this saying scarcely expresses desire, if not under the guise of domination of the world by the logos – a sort of theoretical passion. A mastery by meaning supplants a culture of life: of breath and desire. The proof of masculine power is assessed through the ability to be wise. The supreme Deity would henceforth be impassive and neuter and, under his supremacy, secondary divinities, both good and bad, would organize themselves. Man has tried to master without taking the time to tame.

The negative, in particular, does not yet reach the status that it should acquire in order to respect the other as other. Man intuitively understands that he must confront it. But he is not yet able to make use of the negative towards himself in order to live himself as a limited being leaving room for the other, in particular woman, and for what will always elude his experience, notably in knowledge. Man fails to imagine that the world that he constructs is a partial world: his own and nothing but his own. And that other worlds exist with which he mixes without recognizing them. In his world, he will thus experience the good and the bad, the visible and the invisible, the awakened and the asleep, the living and the dead, the permanent and the impermanent, etc. But he does not realize the relative nature of such experiences. No more does he understand that the One which he gives himself to unify them beyond their contrasts and oppositions is neither absolute nor neuter, but the one that he works out from what or who he is. It could be otherwise only if he had raised the negative itself to a transcendental level, without making it correspond to any being whatsoever. The negative then becomes the absolutely irreducible which lies between the other and him – and, first, between woman and man.

To conceive the negative in this way has a decisive impact on the way of thinking and living. The opposition between life and death, for example, acquires a different meaning. My life is at every moment limited by the life of the other, which implies a certain death. However, the life of the other brings me a surplus of life if I respect this other as different. Life and death are thus no longer opposed to one another in an absolute way but keep alive a relation, that is in some way dialectical, which transforms both their meaning and their lived experience. Such a dialectic also modifies the opposition between the one and the multiple by favouring the relation between two, two who are different, between which a dialectical process can exist. This process restructures the relation between the one and the multiple, the multiple being ceaselessly and thoroughly worked out by a dialectic between – n times – two terms, that the assumption of the negative by each one maintains in their unity and difference(s), while ensuring their transformation thanks to the relation between them. Likewise, the opposition between mortal and immortal is modified because of the constant relation to an other, irreducibly different from me, through and in whom somehow I die, though acquiring in this way a permanence, a sort of immortality here and now. This is not the case if I merge in the multiple, which will then perhaps acquire a certain historical continuity but at the expense of a personal human becoming.

The assumption of the negative as an absolute provides each life at once with an establishment and a limit. This insuperable transcendence of the negative is what can release daily existence and its language from supposedly real and empirical oppositions, thanks to which man has attempted to be situated in the world, to say what he was experiencing of it and to organize it into a whole.

The fact that the philosopher tries to apprehend the whole through opposites is a sign of the insistence of a negative that has not found the place where it ought to work – Being itself. It is not outside of Being, such as it is determined by man, that the negative should be expelled through a good choice carried out between the opposites or alternations under which life or the world appear to him. Such a Being should instead become worked by the negative, that is to say by the fact that it is not the whole of Being, that its relation to Being is partial. Man is not the whole of being, and it is not by projecting this whole onto an absolute Being that he will free himself from being split between multiple oppositions, external as well as internal to himself. He then entrusts his reunification to a beyond able to reconcile opposites or alternations without being himself the architect of the overcoming of a negative that he projected onto everything, for lack of recognizing that it concerns him. This would require that he take care differently of the real of his birth and existence as being at once autonomous and partial. Absolute in its partiality.

It is by taking charge of myself as a unique existence, separated from every other, but also as an existence that does not represent the whole of the world, and first of all the whole of humanity, that I can constitute myself as unity, a unity that is partial and in relation with other partial unities. These unities among which I am placed cannot form a Unity, a Whole, because they are different and non-complementary. Each existence, if it accepts itself as specific and not reducible to any other or to an undifferentiated human existence, can compose a whole which evolves but never reaches a Whole identical to that of other existences. And neither can it compose a unified Whole with them. Experiencing the totality must remain a singular experience which cannot be shared as such. This experience can be exceeded by the experience of the totality of the other without being able to form a single One, a single Whole with it. Between the two wholes, between the world of the one and that of the other, subsists and must subsist a real that belongs neither to the one nor to the other and which allows the relation between the two to be without subjection of the one to the other. This real – be it nature or desire – must remain fluid, free, and can be neither mastered nor enclosed by any particular world.

The binary oppositions that found Western logic result, to a great extent, from a will to master the fluid – what is elusive, not reducible to a name, to an object, to any totalization, but can ensure the cohesion of a whole, in particular thanks to the negative. The fluid is of a more tactile than visual, or even auditory, nature, even if it intervenes in the exercise of all our senses, including the two senses privileged in the elaboration of our theoretical universe. For want of considering the decisive role that the fluid plays in a thinking of the living, the fluid has been left in the darkness of Western culture.

The natural origin, the maternal origin, has more connection to the fluid and to the tactile than to the apparent, to the visible. It has thus been confused with the darkness – good or bad depending on whether this origin was experienced in a positive or negative way. However that may be, it remained removed from the sight, from the light of Western reason. And this was accompanied by nostalgia, hatred, contempt, at the very least by fear, tinged with reverence or rejection – sentiments equally tied, subsequently, to god(s).

The invisible of our begetting has been assimilated to the night of the world of man. Instead of being recognized and respected as an attribute of the being of woman, irreducible and unknowable by man, it has been compared, and even confused, with a state of nature that man should learn to dominate: the darkness, or has been considered extraneous to Being: that which cannot be seen, thought or said in the logic of man.

The forgetting of an elusive origin

The emphasis put on genealogy and on good or bad modalities of engendering results from the inability of man to imagine that he is only a part of humanity – in relation with a different part with which he must come to terms and conceive without it being knowable by him. This means in an obscure and nocturnal manner in comparison to his way of perceiving being.

Conflict between genealogies, with excesses corresponding to each one, has been substituted for the recognition of the irreducible and fecund difference between man and woman. A difference that requires one to have access to a relation to the negative that is transcendental and not confused with the more or less positive or negative affects that express themselves in the living experience or discourse linked to genealogical ties. A lack of human articulation between nature and culture at the level of difference between the sexes has meant that the concern with natural engendering could only be ambivalent, all the more so since the dual origin of this engendering had no possible expression in the logic that was established.

This duality, invisible as such in the connection that it implies, has perhaps reappeared under the form of ambivalence and couplings of opposites in a culture where the beginning remains tied to natural engendering, on the one hand, and is subjected, on the other hand, to a tradition structured starting from an Absolute that is situated beyond our earthly possibilities and that privileges what is created with respect to what is engendered. In the first case, man searches for his path through wandering, suffering, ambiguity, and through the attempt to invent by himself a language parallel to the living world that allows him to master it. In the other case, man considers himself to be the creature of a God who imposes upon him the path from a beyond that he will reach only after death without ever being able to fulfill it. In the one, she – and She – is at the beginning; in the other, he – and especially He – is at the origin of a world created outside of a natural engendering, a world in which creatures are organized in a hierarchical manner in relation to an absolute model. These two universes seem to join up at a certain time while maintaining a difference of interpretation regarding the origin of the Absolute – sometimes being the fruit of a human thought, sometimes being of a purely divine nature.

What these two cultures have not imagined or considered is that our origin is dual. We are engendered by two – two who are different – but the relation between these two, of whom we are born, is neither representable nor sayable as such. This nothing that would lie at the origin has been thought as chaos, yawning gap, absence of words, nothingness, even inert matter. It would then be situated on the side of a maternal beginning, the foundation of which one would always search for backwards – depths opening more and more upon depths beyond all limit. Or it would instead be on the side of the father that the aporia of our origin would reappear – a father creating us from nothing, giving us life starting from a supposedly inanimate matter.

Two interpretations of the world, two cultures have been worked out in a parallelism that sometimes has given rise to oppositions and conflicts, and sometimes to crossings between the one and the other, indeed to reductions of one to the other. If we find in Hesiod, for example, an intuition of the importance of Eros as the inaugural divinity of cosmogony, later traditions hardly imagined that our being could be the fruit of the amorous relation between two, and not of one or the other of the parts of a couple. Privileging sometimes one and sometimes the other of these parts, our culture has led to hypostasizing either desire and love, particularly carnal love, or speech, from both our individual existence and our meetings. From then on, we have made our way from an origin sinking into an abyss: in a night without words, passions without limits, a nature left uncultivated or a logos without flesh, abstract discourses, a divine wanting in soul.

We are orphaned from what brought us into the world – the union between two different humans and worlds. This difference can be perceived in terms of opposites or oppositions only if one extrapolates the duality from what constitutes it as duality, if one abstracts the couple who engenders from its natural and spiritual existence in order to reduce such a couple to categories within a logical framework. In this case, the union between those who are different, who have become opposites, is never restored, except through resorting to a supernatural universe in which difference no longer exists.

The couple who engendered cannot amount to a dualism of matter and form, night and day, earth and sky, etc. – but nor to woman and man thought in terms of logical categories. Conceiving is never the fruit of an opposition except within a world parallel to the real and living world, a world elaborated by a single part of humanity, independently of its first reality and truth, always tied to the couple that it forms with the other part.

The elusiveness of the relation that engendered us has been mistaken for the night in which we lived our gestation in and with the mother. The ambivalence towards the nocturnal has been attributed to the mother – the one in whom we became living bodies, the one who carried and nourished us before, but also after, our coming into the world, our coming to see, and to perceive in a conscious and thoughtful manner. The fecund night of union between two materially and spiritually different worlds has not ruled over our origin because it is unthinkable according to our categories. The aura of being and Being from which it engenders and envelops us, before any real conception, has been neglected, ignored, in the dark. An obscurity that results from the invisible from which we come – the one that is at the origin of our conception and that we have projected beyond our earthly existence.

In the beginning was what attracts one towards the other – preceding the one and the other as separated, but born of the one and the other as different. In the beginning is the attraction, a movement of nature more tactile than visual, which urges us to search for our accomplishment in and with the other. That it is there above all a question of our proper realization, and this can only happen with the other, has remained unthought. Even the intuition of this truth has been covered over by gods, engendering, couplings of opposites, ideal entities, etc. There only remained the night that we envision too little as mystery of a difference or a union, but rather as wandering or ambivalence vis-à-vis a mother who has given us a visible existence starting from a nocturnal sojourn in her. But this duality already hides what is invisible in the relation of which we are born. Hence, perhaps, our ambiguous feelings towards the one who represents a part of our origin – the one who gives us a body, nourishment and even breath and love, but does not reveal to us that we are born of two – hyphen, symbol, seal of a union between two who are different who aspires to an impossible return to our conception.

Unless we grow, renounce the nostalgia for a regression to the origin, in order to become able to seal, in turn, a union with the different. Not a union willed, and somehow imposed, by others – those who, one way or another, have engendered or created us, but a union willed by us, and sealed by an exchange of words freely given to one another.

In this would consist, in fact, the passage to a new stage of human becoming. We find traces of such an attempt in our cultural tradition. Thus for the oath founded on blood ties – Horkos – Dike tried to substitute a justice that arbitrates the bonds created by an exchange of words freely granted, by a promise, a pact, an accord between different humans capable of committing themselves to one another at the level of speech.

For Dike, there would not be, in the beginning, an opposition between blood ties and the bonds sealed through an exchange of words. Dike would represent a will to join them with each other, which requires an ability to emancipate oneself from a mere dependence on the verticality of genealogy, on blood ties, to freely create a horizontal bond with another human, with other humans. The fundamental paradigm of such bonds lies in the free exchange of words between adult women and men, sealing a commitment between them.

At that time – and still today – this stage of human accomplishment is not really attained. Speech has been appropriated only on the side of man, leaving woman in a natural status, still deprived of any voice. A just alliance between women and men had not yet occurred. An alliance that allows the fecundity of their difference to engender not only at the level of nature but also at that of culture. An alliance capable of refounding on more equitable and universal bases the so-called private life, and its family unit, as well as what is called public life. An alliance in which different identities and worlds join together, without abolishing their duality, with a view towards giving birth to a more just, more loving and happier future.

For lack of such an alliance, we see, at that time, the gods seizing young mortal women, in order to engender in them their descendants, preferably male, and men creating a culture or society of between-men, women being excluded from the city and reduced to a private property confined within the family home. And we see, still today, the logos attributed to a God-the-Father to impose its authority on the whole of humanity, and the older men, be it only culturally, mating, whether legally or not, with younger women to make of them their spouse and the mother of their children or merely their lover, admission to public life being moreover reserved for women able to appear as men or to integrate into the customs, language and culture of men elaborated on their exclusion.

The importance of respecting and cultivating natural life has gradually been forgotten in favour of appearances, doing or acting like, words and habits, more or less arbitrary in relation to the real, in which humanity loses sight of its origin: the mysterious and elusive union between two different living human beings, man and woman.

Before being capable of remembering this event, unrepresentable according to our logic, and resuming the journey of a human becoming not based on forgetting, it is necessary, for us, to cross back over a culture constructed from the necessities of the unique – one, identical, same, equal, etc. – masculine subject and find again the one who was in the beginning: the mother.

It is essential to allow this mother to emerge from the lack of differentiation from nature where man placed her, and to affirm that a different identity exists, that of a woman, an identity with which man must come to terms to build a truly human world.

5

Between myth and history: The tragedy of Antigone

The tragedy suffered by Antigone takes place between a myth and its possible embodiment in History. It is the difficulty of unveiling the meaning of Antigone's will and act, and the resistance of our History to their realization, that explain why Antigone remains such a persistent myth in our tradition. I will not cite here the names of all the prestigious creators who have shown an interest in Antigone, a figure who generally appeals to them but sometimes also repulses them. Their interpretations are usually too psychological, egological, indeed narcissistic, to correspond to that epoch in which Antigone's character entered into our culture. In those ancient Greek times, specular or speculative reflection did not yet exist, nor a subject as such who may be concerned by them. The habitual manner of approaching

Antigone's character transforms it into a feminine subjectivity, a sort of eternal feminine, situated within what is really a later tradition in which psychology and sociology lay down the law and are used as methods of interpretation. But Antigone has little to do with these more or less recent understandings, which often amount to the projections of men into or onto the mystery that woman remains for them, a mystery that they do not want to consider and respect as such; that is, as the sign of a belonging to another identity, to another world and culture than their own, which our Western tradition has repressed, indeed forgotten. The persistence of Antigone's character is linked to our History more than the usual interpretations claim, even though it has not yet entered into History and still represents today a question put to the Western historical tradition concerning its development from a certain epoch onward.

Sharing Antigone's tragic fate

Since *Speculum*, and even before, I have been interested in Antigone. I have been fortunate enough – certainly it has been a painful lot to endure – to experience exclusion because I tried to unveil truth, notably regarding Antigone. Anyway, it is revealing that the numerous essays concerning this character which have been published after *Speculum*, in particular those written by men, ordinarily do not cite my interpretation nor other interpretations which in one way or another follow the same lines as, for example, that of Clémence Ramnoux relating to the evolution of early Greek culture or, in part, that of Johann Jakob Bachofen concerning matriarchy – Bachofen who they say inspired Hegel himself and of whom he was a presumed cousin. This is a sign of the resistance to recognizing the truth that Antigone conveys and of refusing the possible entry of such a truth into History.

Hence the continuation of the tragedy, the continuation of fate as the Greeks said, in the life of the one who upholds such a truth. I have shared Antigone's tragic fate: the exclusion from socio-cultural places because of my public assertion of a truth that has been repressed, or at least not recognized as such, and that thus disturbs our usual order. Fortunately, if I have been excluded from society – from universities, psychoanalytical institutions, circles of scientists and even of friends, in part from publishing houses and, more recently, from my house itself – I have not been deprived of my relation to the natural world. Expelled from public organizations, enclosed or shrouded within a silence that I sometimes felt to be the opaque wall of a tomb, I have not been deprived of my relation to air, to the sun, to the plant and animal worlds. I have been expelled from the polis, the city, the human society to which I belonged and sent back to the natural world that my contemporaries no longer appreciate or consider of much value, and hence something of which it was unnecessary to deprive me.

Being sent back to the natural world in this way has allowed me to survive or, better, to rediscover what life itself is. Furthermore, it helped me to unearth that Greek world in which Antigone's character appeared, and to perceive the meaning of her tragic destiny.

In contrast to Hegel's thinking as well as that of most commentators on Antigone's tragedy, and furthermore in contrast to a large number of feminists, I did not imagine – like Antigone herself – that coming into conflict with men could solve my tragic destiny or, at least, I quickly understood that such conflicts were useless. The matter was, the matter still is, one of entering another time of History, reviving the message of Antigone and pursuing its embodiment in our culture. But for this we need first to realize that the two periods of time which come into conflict in Sophocles' tragedy, the two discourses that alternate between one another, that reply to each other without any mutual understanding, belong to two different worlds whose difference has to be respected without intending to incorporate them into the higher unity of a single world. This requires us to embody the negative in a way other than that which is usual in our tradition. Thus, in Hegel's system, the negative serves to overcome a subjective and an objective scission in two with a view to oneness. In my own thinking, the negative has become insuperable and serves to maintain the existence of the duality of subjects and of their worlds, between whom the question is now one of constructing a culture without abolishing either the one or the other. This implies that we relinquish our logic based on pairs of opposites at the service of oneness, and enter a logic of coexistence and dialogue between two different subjects and worlds. I could add that this demands that we invent another dramatic play through which we can relate to each other as different.

It is thus with the aid of my own experience, of my own destiny – to which even my psychoanalyst sent me back – and in particular with the help of a tragic solitude that I will propose my interpretation of the figure of Antigone. I have already presented certain aspects of it in some of my writings, but I will now resume my meditation on Antigone's character, notably in connection with my own life and my own work, and develop some traits of this character that I had not yet elaborated and that seem to me necessary for understanding both Antigone's way of acting and the perpetuation of her myth as a truth which is insistent but remains veiled.

In my current interpretation of the duty carried out by Antigone, I will distance myself more from Hegel than I did in the chapter 'The Eternal Irony of the Community' devoted to Antigone in *Speculum*. Because I have been expelled from social places, from the belonging on which Hegel founded his reading of Sophocles' tragedy, because in a way I have been buried alive in the natural world, and also because the truth that I tried to unveil, after arousing enthusiasm and bedazzlement, has again been covered and hidden by the arbitrary and subsequent blindness of our civilization, the mystery that envelops Antigone has become more familiar to me, indeed more intimate. It also shed light on the way for me to go deeper into an interpretation of patriarchal tradition as well as towards the elaboration of a logic or a dialectics in the feminine that could enable women to enter into relations with men without renouncing their own subjectivity and world, their own path.

No doubt my practice of yoga and my approach to Eastern traditions have allowed me to envision and value Antigone's rationality and wisdom in contrast to Creon's irrationality and madness. Sophocles' tragedy takes place in the passage from a manner of thinking faithful to life, love and desire towards a reasoning which leads only to destruction, hatred and death. There are many signs of such a passage in Sophocles' tragedy, for example, in the allusions and invocations to certain gods, in the words of the chorus or the omens of the soothsayer.

I have been, like Antigone herself, criticized for disturbing the established order in the name of personal passions. I would like to make clear that I spoke and acted in the name of an order repressed in our tradition, an order that it is necessary to consider again with the becoming and accomplishment of humanity in mind. To come back to Antigone, she in no way wills the perturbation of the order of the city, but she has to obey a higher order, unwritten laws, which the new order, embodied by Creon in Sophocles' tragedy, intended to abolish.

The law or the duty Antigone defends at the risk of her life includes three aspects that are linked together: respect for the order of the living universe and living beings, respect for the order of generation and not only genealogy, and respect for the order of sexuate difference. It is important to stress the word 'sexuate,' and not 'sexual,' because the duty of Antigone does not concern sexuality as such, nor even its restraint as Hegel thought. If this was the case, she ought to have privileged her fiancé Hemon and not her brother. Antigone undertakes the burial of her brother because he represents a singular concrete sexuate identity that must be respected as such: 'as the son of her mother.' For Antigone, human identity has not yet become one, neuter, universal as Creon's order will render it. Humanity is still two: man and woman, and this duality, already existent in the natural order, must be respected, as a sort of frame, before the fulfillment of sexual attraction or desire. What Antigone sustains is the necessity of respecting her brother as brother before wedding Hemon. She explains that without placing herself in relation to the different sexuate identity of her brother, she cannot marry another man, and while she could not substitute any one for her brother, this brother being unique for her, she could marry another man. She thus has to protect her dead brother from the derision and from the decay of being eaten away, from the regression to animality through being devoured by birds of prey or other carnivores, from endless wandering as a ghost deprived of burial. She must secure for her brother the memory of a valid sexuate identity, and not just of an anonymous and neutralized bodily matter.

Respect for life and cosmic order

Thus the first law that Antigone obeys concerns respect for the cosmic order. It is important to understand that cosmos, for the Greeks, refers to a comprehensive order that includes nature and living beings, the gods and humans. It is, then, not a question of an undifferentiated natural world, as Western culture imagines after it has destroyed the cosmic order that previously existed.

Sophocles' tragedy tells us about the passage from the harmony of a cosmic order to a fabricated human world, a world that no longer takes into consideration an established harmony between living nature, gods and humans. The duty that Antigone attempts to accomplish is that of preserving the equilibrium of the cosmic order, notably with regard to the difficult relations between Zeus and Hades, the god of light and the god of darkness or shadow, who will later be called the god of the heavens and the god of the underworld. To give burial to Polynices means trying to maintain a delicate balance between the two gods, the two worlds. It is not to favour the god of the underworld – as has too often been said in relation to the character of Antigone, and firstly by Creon himself – but to endeavour not to break a possible passage between the two worlds, a passage that not only the dead brother needs but also, more generally, the harmony of the whole cosmos. Antigone's gesture intends to venerate Zeus as much as Hades and to maintain a fragile harmony between the two gods and their mutual realms.

Only because of the failure of her attempt to bury Polynices according to the rite of passage from an earthly sojourn to the sojourn of the dead, does Antigone talk about sharing Persephone's destiny. Persephone is the name given to Kore after she has been taken away from her mother, the great goddess Demeter, by the god of the underworld. This sacrificial rape of his virgin daughter was accepted by Zeus himself in order to re-establish a possible cosmic order, notably thanks to a link with his brother Hades.

It seems that the death sentence Creon pronounces on Antigone repeats in a way the sacrificial removal of a virgin from the earthly maternal sojourn and leaves her without any dwelling either on earth or in the underworld, either with living beings or with the dead. But, as Antigone asserts, this time Zeus himself is no longer the one responsible for her removal from the earthly sojourn or life; the one responsible is now Creon, who appeals to Zeus in a way that breaks the cosmic harmony. This appeal to the omnipotence of Zeus, to the detriment of considering the total cosmic harmony between gods, humans and all living beings, then begins to rule Western culture and to lead it to possible chaos and destruction.

This is announced by the chorus, which tells of a desire of man for mastery, a desire that endangers cosmic harmony and can sometimes result in a bad situation or nothing, sometimes in the achievement of brave deeds. The chorus says that man's thirst for dominating the sea, for taming wild animals and breaking-in horses and bulls, his wish to understand everything through words, his capability to escape bad weather by building houses and to rule over cities, show an arrogance that defies the gods and could provoke their wrath. The chorus explains how man intends to bring the earth, the noblest of the gods, into submission and work her until exhaustion. The chorus talks about man as a clever manufacturer who lacks experience, and seeks to master all, including the power of the gods, but is unable to escape death. The chorus describes how man has lost the possibility of dwelling because he only dominates and overlooks his place on earth without living in it. And the chorus, which is presumed to represent the people, invokes the words: 'may such a man never frequent my hearth, and my mind never share the presumption of the one who acts this way.'

Some commentators wonder whether these words refer to Creon or to Antigone. In my opinion, they can only allude to Creon and the culture in the masculine that he inaugurates. In contrast to Creon, Antigone fights to maintain cosmic harmony: not to provide her brother with burial harms nature itself, notably the air and the sun. The question is not only of ensuring a personal passage for Polynices from the earth to the underworld but of caring about the balance between the cosmic elements, of which divinities are the guardians.

And Antigone is not the only person who claims respect for the cosmic order. The soothsayer – like the chorus – talks in the same way. The soothsayer tells how he heard barbarous calls of birds previously unknown and saw the birds killing one another; furthermore, he tells how no sacrifice could restore peace and harmony because the flame did not arise from his offerings. All this means that both the heavens and the underworld are polluted because Polynices' flesh has remained without the appropriate ritual and has been left to birds of prey and wild dogs.

The lack of a burial for Polynices harms life itself for all living beings, breaking the economy of relations between earth and sky, air and sun. At that time, providing burial first had to do with respecting earthly harmony and the atmosphere depending on it. Caring about the burial of Polynices is certainly a religious gesture on Antigone's part, but 'religious' is here endowed with a meaning that differs from what we now attribute to this word. It is not a question of being submitted to the law of one unique God, whom we have to join in heaven, but of being concerned with maintaining balance in the cosmic order by caring about the living world that surrounds us.

Unfortunately we, Westerners, usually forget to consider as religious the concern for cosmic order. We can even harm the world through bombs, indeed atomic bombs, if it is in the name and in the service of our God, this is a religious act. This behaviour is irreligious from Antigone's point of view but not from the point of view of many monotheists, who consider it valid to destroy the living world, including humans as living beings, in order to defend their belief in an eternal reality.

Is irrationality, then, to be found on the part of Antigone or on the part of monotheistic people? On which side is madness, and on which side wisdom? And could it be because man wanted everything at once and only for himself that such a God has been created by him? What can be shared with man when he has faith only in his God? God himself? But this God is not shareable by all humans in the whole world. He is presumed to be the absolute for everyone. Perhaps he has been the absolute for men of our culture. It is not even certain that the God of monotheism can correspond to the absolute for a woman of this culture who is faithful to herself. Perhaps her absolute is closer to that of Antigone. At the very least, it requires respect for the unwritten laws that Antigone defends. Could a divine absolute in the feminine exist before the respect for our duties concerning life itself? Could it impose its law on life itself, or substitute itself for life? Becoming divine in the feminine takes place beyond simply living: it amounts to accomplishing life and making it blossom, and does not have to do with something existing instead of life, indeed against life, as God has too often been understood in our tradition.

Antigone cannot reach this stage of divine fulfillment because the law concerning life is not respected: with regard to cosmic order, with regard to generational order, with regard to sexuate order. She was waiting for the divine blossoming of her life, of her love. But this could only happen after a respect for and a cultivation of her living surroundings, after giving thanks to those who brought her into the world, after securing a valid memory for her brother. Without taking into account the unwritten laws regarding these dimensions of our existence, she cannot attain another level in becoming divine.

Antigone knows this, and she cannot fulfill her desire for Hemon, her fiancé, without first providing for Polynices' burial. There is no blind or adolescent passion in this, but a deep consideration for unwritten laws regarding life. Blind passion would be to marry her fiancé before discharging her duty with respect to life. Her respect for such laws preserves her autonomy and her feminine world, and prevents her from becoming a mere function or role in the patriarchal world then beginning to impose its order, at least the one that Creon represents.

Antigone cannot submit to the arbitrary laws on which Creon founds his power – that is, to a basically nihilist order – because she defends life and its values. Rather than being subjected to death drives, as it has been said, Antigone struggles to preserve living beings and their dwelling. She cannot accept survival instead of living. She loves life and the living world, living beings. Even Jean Anouilh, who does not understand a great deal about Antigone, talks of her love for the garden before dawn, when no human has yet looked at it, and of her concern for her dog after her death. Her love for the sun, as giving light and warmth to living beings, compels her to give burial to her brother although in doing so she runs the risk of being sentenced to death by the king Creon. The sun, like the air, takes part in the dwelling of living beings on earth, and Antigone has to care about them.

It is precisely the air and the sun that the king will deprive her of; that is, the living world that she needs to live. He tries to avoid an act forbidden by the law; he tries to kill without overtly killing, depriving Antigone of the surroundings that permit her to live, without actually murdering her and refusing her body burial.

In a way, all of our Western patriarchal system amounts to this: killing without openly committing a murder; that is to say, little by little depriving us of the surroundings that allow us to live, by polluting, annihilating the equilibrium of the environment, destroying the plant and animal worlds, and finally humanity itself. And it may happen that people then prefer to take their own life rather than waiting for a complete imbalance of our planet that does not permit them to quietly pursue their survival. This may happen, and this really does happen, as we know. People, in this way, somehow anticipate a death planned by the patriarchal economy, which often only grants us survival and not life itself.

To such a state of merely surviving, Antigone says: no. Can we then talk about a desire for dying, or about a love for life? Is it not surviving at any cost that testifies to a wish to die rather than to really live? This choice does not suit Antigone. The supreme value for her is life. No other value can substitute for it: no abstract ideal, no truth or absolute. And she is not waiting for another life in another world, beyond her earthly sojourn. It is here and now that she desires to live and share life, not later, beyond her present dwelling. If Antigone cares about her dead brother, it is not because she takes a particular interest in the dead, as has often been said. She wants to preserve life.

Antigone does not ask for this or that, she only asks to live, to be. What has been described, indeed condemned, as Antigone's passion for the absolute is instead an outward sign of her desire to live, to be. She is not fighting in the name of an absolute that is external to her, but for living, for being.

Each living being is an absolute insofar as it remains faithful to life. Life needs one to keep oneself whole and not to become some thing or some reality onto which one projects one's passion. It is not true that Antigone wants all at once, an all external to her, or to die. She wants to be the whole that she is as a living being. And it is true that if she gives up being this whole, she will die, in one way or another. She wants to live and not to die. To be and remain as a living being does not require possessing some things or others, but rather being a someone.

Respect for generational order

To be a living being needs a certain surrounding world: it is not possible without air, water, but also the light and warmth of the sun, and the fertility of the earth. To be someone really living also calls for limits. Limits are provided by the necessities of life itself, among other things its surroundings, but also by relations with other living beings, in particular those of one's own species. Relational limits between humans are provided through genealogy and sexuate difference.

Genealogy is here endowed with a meaning different from that to which we are accustomed. We generally understand genealogy within the horizon of the patriarchal tradition, especially, but not only, regarding the organization of the family. The main cause of the tragedy of Antigone, and one of its teachings, is that patriarchy has been established in an arbitrary and repressive manner. Instead of attempting to achieve an alliance between maternal and paternal genealogies, one has tried to supplant the other. However, each one contributes to culture in a specific way and with specific values.

The maternal genealogy favours the values of life, of generation, of growth. It is based on unwritten laws that do not clearly distinguish civil order from religious order. It does not attach an absolute importance to family as such, as patriarchy does. It privileges daughters and, later, the youngest son as heirs. This privilege is founded in relation to the perpetuation of generation itself and not the inheritance of goods, functions, or names.

It is obvious that Antigone tries to be faithful to a maternal order or culture that Creon is destroying, erasing, through an arbitrary power, arbitrary laws and discourses. Beyond her concern for life itself, Antigone cares about her youngest brother, the one who does not inherit power in a paternal genealogy, but is 'the son of her mother.' Other things bear witness to the values of a maternal genealogy: of course the words of the chorus and those of the soothsayer, but also an unusual beginning in the tragedy, a conversation between two sisters who, furthermore, embody the dilemma between faithfulness to maternal values or subjection to the power of Creon. It is interesting to note that, in their exchange, the middle voice is initially used – a Greek verbal form which expresses that the two have a part, even if differently, in the same whole – and that this form disappears after their division between two traditions, two genealogies.

The reason put forward to justify the repression of the maternal order is that incest was frequent in such a tradition. I, for one, do not believe this. Rather, the generalized practice of incest takes place after the emergence of a contempt for the unwritten laws of the maternal order, an order renowned for its ethics and in which it is obvious to all who the mother is. What can then happen is love outside the family ruled by patriarchal power. The revered goddess is Aphrodite rather than Hera, the divinity who presides over the patriarchal family and who only with difficulty relates to Aphrodite, a goddess who resists the confinement of love in the new family institution.

In the tragedy of Antigone, the chorus alludes to Aphrodite as the goddess who governs alongside the masters of the world, and is capable of breaking up the patriarchal family in the name of desire and love. These invocations-to and praise-of Aphrodite occur after the rebellion of Hemon against his father Creon because of his love, his desiring love, for the virgin Antigone.

According to the chorus, Aphrodite is the one who is victorious in the murderous confrontations of this tragedy in which, in spite of the death of Antigone and Hemon, desire and love win out over the power that tries to submit them to new institutional bounds.

In fact, Aphrodite, like the maternal tradition, respects an ethical order, at least originally. Desire and love, desire as love, then, obey certain laws that, along with the greatest laws, take part in the government of the world. Incest, which would be the cause of the tragedy suffered by Antigone, does not result from the maternal order or that of Aphrodite. Rather it comes from a regression to undifferentiation provoked by a truly problematic establishment of patriarchy. It is then that the mother loses her identity and lovers their difference.

To the best of my knowledge and information, Oedipus' incest is neither unique nor singular. It represents a figure or character that appears with the culture then beginning. Because he wants to annihilate maternal and feminine identity and values, man falls back into a lack of differentiation and chaos with respect to his origin and attractions. The world that he constructs through his logic is parallel to the original natural world that he intends to dominate. But this division between a supposed nature and its mastery by masculine culture results in two artificial and in some way neuter universes that no longer correspond to a living real and its cultivation, beginning with the real that man is. Incest, then, can be understood as a nostalgic regression to an initial state, and culture as an attempt to emerge from it, with all the ambivalences that accompany such movements. On no account does the possibility of attaining an identity of his own exist, and man continues to claim it from two worlds which lack differentiation because he fabricated them through the annihilation of maternal and feminine difference. His quest leads him from a regressive incestuous return to a neutralization in a someone or a somebody who differs from others only through goods or power; and this in some way amounts to an indirect incestuous behaviour.

The exile from his first natural identity and sojourn leaves man lost and blind in the artificial world that he created. And such a blindness seems to suit him. After knowing that he made love with his mother, Oedipus puts out his eyes instead of learning to henceforth consider the person who appeals to him. He does not learn from his mistake to address and modify his lack of perception of the other: rather, he chooses to increase the risk of being mistaken by gouging out his eyes. He reduplicates his blindness instead of trying to become one who is now capable of seeing. He does not want to renounce being attracted to the mother, an attraction that corresponds to longing for a blind tactile sharing with the maternal world in which difference is still lacking and passive sensations are predominant in well-being.

It is not a mere coincidence that Antigone became Oedipus' guide after he lost his sight. Antigone recognizes the difference between her father and her beloved because she respects the law concerning life and generation. She knows that she has to take the living order into consideration before wedding Hemon. Fulfilling her desire without first respecting life, its environment and generational conditions, does not enter the ethical world of Antigone.

Respect for sexuate differentiation

Furthermore, nature as such lets many differences arise, grow and bloom. Nature itself is not lacking in differences, as the Western masculine tradition, which has intended to master it, claims. On the contrary, nature is more differentiated than the world built by man, and it requires an order that the earliest Greek culture tried to respect. Natural differences are also less hierarchical because each remains faithful to its own origin, growth and blossoming and is not standardized through its submission to one unique world that knows only quantitative differences.

Humans live among different beings if they remain respectful of their natural surroundings. The human species includes within itself its differentiation, its difference, because it is formed by two. To use this duality exclusively to reproduce is not specifically human, whereas to make difference the place of access to transcendence, a transcendence inscribed in nature itself, seems to fit human beings as such.

The place where human difference appears is between sister and brother. In our tradition man as such does not differentiate himself enough from the maternal world, or from a neuter individual of the polis, the state. Husband and wife are, paradoxically, not distinguished by their different identities but by different functions in reproductive and parental responsibilities.

They are at the service of nature, but only in terms of the survival of the human species. Sexuate identity is not what characterizes the couple in our traditional family. And perhaps Hegel was mistaken on this point, at least in part. He remains within the horizon of his primitive family as a son, rather than situating himself in relation to the family that he founded as a husband. Indeed, this family perhaps did not yet exist, and perhaps does not yet exist today.

Hegel mistakes – as does Sophocles in his tragedy, but with another intention – man with Creon or Oedipus and woman with Antigone or Ismene, taking into consideration only sexuate roles or functions and not sexuate identity as such. He places man in a political role without a real sexuate identity. So Creon affirms his male identity through an arbitrary order and not through an identity of his own that implicates a specific relation to immanence and transcendence. In a way, Creon is a eunuch, as Oedipus is, but in a different manner. They have both sacrificed their sexuate identity to a lack of differentiation from the maternal world: merging in it or rebelling against it, notably through misogyny. But that does not suffice for reaching and accomplishing an identity of one's own.

Antigone is the one who testifies that a sexuate identity exists and has to be respected. And if she defends the generational order it is also because it lets sexuate identity appear. But not between husband and wife, who are destined to become mother and father, but between sister and brother, the place where it appears that neither the mother nor the father could represent a unique and neuter origin, whether it results from natural or fabricated undifferentiation. Between sister and brother, genealogy becomes the generation of two different horizontal identities: appearance of the transcendence of sexuate identity with respect to the body.

Our natural belonging then supplies a transcendence to a mere material belonging or undifferentiation in relation to all living beings, including humans. And it is no longer necessary to repress our natural origin in order to reach culture. It provides us with a cultural horizon: the transcendence of our sexuate identity, which is not only a bodily identity but also a cultural identity because it creates a world different for man and woman.

To give burial to Polynices amounts, on Antigone's part, to preserving a transcendental world not only as the world of the dead but firstly as the world of her brother, that is, of an identity different from her own. This other world remains invisible: it delimits a horizon within which it is not possible to see. This does not mean that it is merely night or even the underworld, but that it remains irreducible to the ability to see, understand or substitute of the one who does not belong to the same sexuate being. Of course it is possible to perceive some material sign of difference: the sex organs, for example, but not its meaning for the persons or for the construction of their subjectivity. The way in which the world is formed and organized by a sexuate human is irreducible to the way in which a human of another sex builds his, or her, own world. No one of the two can perceive the world in which the other really dwells: it remains transcendent to him, or her. Recognizing this transcendence permits humanity to emerge from undifferentiation and enter a relational cultural world. The transcendental dimension that exists, or ought to exist, between two differently sexuate persons can provide humanity with a cultural order capable of preventing us from merging or falling back into undifferentiation, notably with regard to the maternal world and any kind of incest that results from an unresolved relation with the maternal origin.

Such a transcendence first appears between sister and brother. Perceiving and respecting it allow us to enter another cultural era faithful to the gesture of Antigone, one which could contribute to the entry of her myth into History. The perception of the transcendence of the world of the other–beginning with the sexuate other, who corresponds to the most basic, universal and irreducible otherness – defines the limits of one's own world, permitting us to pass from a solitary apprehension and construction of the world to a relational cultivation and culture. A solitary world always remains somehow in a natural immediacy. And our Western culture itself partly remains at the level of natural immediacy because it is based on the perception and elaboration of one and the same human, whose sexuate aspects and impact have not been called into question by a differently sexuate one.

Such questioning is recent and compels us to enter a new era starting from a cultivation of the natural immediacy still at work in our culture, on the side of man and of woman. Of course there is no question of returning to a mere natural belonging and of coming into conflict with each other in the name of our different immediate perceptions or feelings. This leads us to a personal and collective regression. And to wars, among others between the sexes, that end in nothing because male and female genders do not amount to the two parts of a single human that could be reached through opposition and conflicts. Male and female genders correspond to two different worlds – and not two roles, functions or characters – irreducible to one another. They have to elaborate a third world through their relations in difference, a third world that does not belong to one or the other, but is generated by the two with respect for their difference(s).

In contrast to Hegel, the question is not to reduce the two to one, but to engender a third starting from the two, whose natural belonging has been cultivated and not abolished or neutralized. The two different worlds do not have to confront each other in order to resolve, cancel or overcome their difference, but have to integrate into their ethical duties the task of forming a new world, taking into account the fecundity of their different belongings. In other words, sexuate belongings are to be taken into consideration to engender a relational culture, and their specificities are not to be ignored so that they unconsciously remain at work in our elaboration of truth and in our practices.

An insurmountable tragedy

To respect our sexuate belonging always partly involves tragedy. Each of us has to embody alone the truth of our own gender; and bringing it forth into History will also remain a tragic gesture, because our sexuate desire longs for the infinite and the absolute while History is limited and human. Furthermore, sexuate truth is and must remain dual, each one having to accomplish alone, with respect for the other, one's sexuate destiny, a destiny that is higher than merely coming into the world as an anonymous body.

To distinguish sexuate belonging from sexual attraction also includes a tragic necessity to which Antigone's ethics bears witness. She needs to recognize the sexuate transcendence of her brother before wedding her beloved. To provide Polynices with burial signifies securing for the sexuate belonging of her brother a permanent, one could say an immortal, status beyond his death. This is needed to protect him both from existing as a mere body, the same as hers, as that of any one, and from being confined to a simple neutralizing role or function: a destiny that the construction of the new Western culture has in store for Creon and Ismene, ahead of all of us. This amounts to an abolition of our difference by a public functionalism which forever prevents us from meeting or wedding together with respect for our real difference.

Fortunately, Antigone resists the decay of our human identity which is then beginning. In texts other than his *Phenomenology of Spirit*, Hegel wonders whether Antigone's mission is not higher than that of Christ himself. Such a question is not without ground. Whatever the comments contrasting the human and the divine could be with regard to Antigone, she defends laws which do not separate civil and religious duties. Of course, this does not mean a form of fundamentalism, because fundamentalism is sociological by nature. Civil duty and religious duty mingle in Antigone's respect for the other as a being transcendent to her, beginning with her brother, the son of her mother.

To pass from singularity to community often leads us to neglect, indeed to forget, the importance of sexuate difference between us. Now this difference, initially and at each time, happens between two different belongings which it provides with limits, to which it brings a sort of death when we pass from natural immediacy to cultural transcendence in relating between us here and now.

This transcendence is universal and can be shared by all people all over the world. It suffices to listen to unwritten laws inscribed in nature itself: the respect for life, for its generation, growth and blossoming and the respect for a sexuate transcendence between us – first of all between children of the same mother, but more generally between all the children of our human species, of our mother nature, whose we are children on this side of or beyond all the more or less artificial sociological constructions that divide us.

6

The return

Why does Western culture have to start with Greece? Why mark such a cut with earlier traditions? With other cultures? What is it to begin with the Greeks? Would it be an emergence of man as such, which also signifies an exile, a wandering, a growing away from home? Does the same go for all cultures? Does knowing necessarily mean an estrangement from oneself? Or does such a knowledge represent only a required historical passage? A kind of journey to come back home. A sort of sojourn abroad in order to appreciate returning to one's own country, one's own land – as Heidegger commented with regard to some of Hölderlin's poems.

But the country, the land and even the house do not yet correspond to the self. Nevertheless, Western tradition keeps alive such a confusion, probably because its culture is mediatized by exteriority without a suitable cultivation of the interiority of the self. And it is also a culture of uprooting from natural origin and belonging. Western culture corresponds to a culture of the outside, not of the inside. We make plans outside us in order to construct, to love, to know, and then we become, in some way, the consequence of events which take place outside us. We are not what gives measure to our culture, except indirectly as a result of going outside of ourselves, and of marks that we make or leave there.

About ourselves, we know almost nothing. And even when we imagine ourselves as constructing the world, it is as much this world which constructs us. Our projects with regard to the world are mostly a projection, and an evasion of ourselves, an escape from ourselves, without a possible turning back to ourselves, in ourselves. In fact, a great part of History amounts to a succession of episodes of our rushing forward to build a world, including a world of knowledge, which little by little substitutes itself for us. A world in which historians will be in search of some traces, some 'skins,' as testimonies of humanity's passage on earth.

Parallel to the estrangement from home, from oneself, we find, in Western culture, the theme of the return. It is not a pure coincidence that the text given as a reference to the earliest Greek culture tells us about both the departure of the hero who is going to war and his eventful journey in turning back home. This double epic gives us an overall picture of our tradition, as do the motive put forward for waging war and the diverse episodes which prevent the hero from returning home. The first part of this prophetic account amounts to the supposedly positive aspect of our culture, and the second part to its negative or reverse side. The first part talks about the emergence of a world of men amongst men, and the second part about the loneliness of the man who tries to return home. He finally succeeds because of his cunning character, but not without undergoing great trials that perhaps mean the stages of a passage from one era of History to another.

The hero goes back home, but does he return to his self? I am not sure. Perhaps he comes back to the order of the hearth, of marriage, but not to the order of his self, to intimacy with his self. And although we hear many things about his relations with female figures outside the home, this is not the case with respect to his wife. We hear of him defeating his wife's suitors through his ruse and his skill with projectiles, which cause people to remember him. But the suitors seem to want the possession of the goods of the hero rather than love as such. In other cultures, we know a lot about amorous rituals, about the comparison of lovers to divine figures, and about the impact of love itself on the cosmic order. With this first epic of Greek culture, love is already becoming an institution bound to the πολι⊠. And lovers already obey external public rules as much as, if not more than, their own affects. They are moving away from nature, from the body, from the economy of affects, and are becoming subjected to external laws.

Nevertheless, the hero still bears witness to self-affection. Ulysses is moved, he weeps, he worries ... and these affects are expressed in the Greek language by the middle-passive or middle voice, a morphological form which expresses that he is affected in himself, with himself, outside of the economy of the pair of opposites: active-passive. This often happens with a certain loneliness, secretly and without an other sharing the affect. The journey of man is not yet deprived of self-affection, but this seems not to provide him with happiness and is lacking in reciprocity.

For what does Western man feel nostalgic?

The journey of Ulysses and his return home happen before the construction of Western metaphysics and announce it. After the end or accomplishment of metaphysics, the theme of the return is insistent again. I could cite Hölderlin and Nietzsche, for example, and comment on their feeling of nostalgia for an impossible return. Both of them have been removed from their own self by Western culture – by a Western culture first embodied in another thinker – and they cannot turn back to this self. As we know, their journey will end in a kind of madness, even though they are each attempting to go back home in a different way. For Hölderlin, the matter is one of again finding familiarity or intimacy with a country, a landscape, a house, and also with friends or a beloved. For Nietzsche, the matter is one of overcoming metaphysics through assuming an eternal return of the same, by bringing it together in a circle. The two are in search of an access to a beyond of metaphysics, but if they announce the necessity of exceeding metaphysics, they do not succeed in such a surpassing of their path, of their history, of their self. The inability to do that comes in part from the lack of a woman who could help them, above all in their self-affecting through love. They thus have both an intuition of the fact that the solution to their ill-being, to their failure in making their way, cannot be found in their cultural background or surroundings as they are, and that something or someone else has to arrive in order to go beyond such a horizon.

Some thinkers thus seek other values, shrouded or forgotten in our culture. But often their plan is one of integrating these values into our culture in order to improve it, without changing themselves. Once more, the question would be of going abroad in order to even more securely stay at home – in one's own country, one's own culture, one's own home. Some also imagine that the solution to the nostalgia for a return might be a perpetual nomadism – an estrangement from home until one forgets what staying at home could be. In the era of globalization that is ours, we can observe two trends: that of the stay-at-homes who try to preserve at all costs their home, country or culture as they are, and that of the nomadic people who denigrate any home. Both of them disregard the relation with the other, which requires an ability to dwell with the possibility of opening oneself to the other, of leaving home to meet with the other while remaining able to return home, to oneself, within oneself in order to keep the two, the one and the other.

Such a going there and back to home, to the self, within the self, is lacking in our tradition, notably because man has searched for himself outside the self and not by making his way in his own self. And also because he has searched for his becoming in objects, things, and their representations or mental reduplications. Man has searched for himself outside the self while intending to appropriate this outside, notably through representations. And this does not represent a cultivation of interiority, but an exile in an external world that he intends to appropriate by means of a technique which reduplicates the real, of a logic through which he makes the world his own, the logos.

Why such a wish? And why has man imagined that the key to the happiness which has been lost, to the unaccomplished blossoming, could be found in his culture, his country, his home or language, and not in a maturity that is still to be reached? Why, above all, has man chosen a culture of performance, of know-how, of mastery, including through language, and not a culture of being-with, of speaking-with; that is, a culture of being in relation with the other? Why has man sacrificed a great part of himself to such a cultural orientation? Why has man immolated affectivity, desire and even life itself to a mental mastery? Why has man compared the evolution of Western consciousness to an inescapable calvary – as Hegel wrote in his *Phenomenology of Spirit*? Probably because man has wanted to give himself a proper identity without caring enough about differentiating himself from the relation with the first human with whom he shared life: his mother. He has sought to master the world before becoming conscious of the first world that he formed with her. They originally lived in the same horizon, without a clear separation between two worlds. It is by dwelling in the same world as her that he was born, has grown, has reached the surrounding environment, the external universe. Western man has not taken into account such a sharing with, and lack of differentiation from, the mother. And neither the logos – a sort of generalized mental bobbin with respect to the world, to speak like Freud – nor the law of a natural, political or spiritual father might allow a passage from the first sensible immediacy of the relation with the mother to a level of perception which can transform it without abolishing it.

Western man has remained in some way confused with the maternal world, stuck to it, and no strategy of Western culture has been able to cultivate this first situation or experience. It stays, one could say, absolute and blind. A sort of maternal incest is generalized in Western culture – as is masculine homosexuality. And the taboos surrounding one and the other are all the more virulent since they are not situated in the place where the question arises.

Thus what does it mean, the insistence on the theme of the return? In particular, what does the present turning back to Greek culture mean? And to what Greek culture are we turning? Are we in search of a completeness that we have lost? Or are we urged on by want of something of which our cultural path has deprived us?

With regard to Greek culture, both are at stake, in my opinion. I think that we are trying to find the crossroads at which we have taken the wrong path. I will attempt to give some indications on this point, starting with the notable disappearance of some morphological forms or meanings that still exist in the earliest Greek culture. As examples, I will take the term ἑτερο⊠, the verbal form called middle-passive or middle voice, and the evolution of the meaning of the word γενο⊠, but also of the value of female or feminine genealogy, all these being accompanied by a loss of a sensible transcendental in the relations with nature and the other, especially the different other.

In the early stages of Greek culture, the word ἑτερο⊠ first of all expresses a relation between only two, two who are different and cannot merge into a one, as is the case in the relation with the mother, and also with God. While the word ἀλλο⊠ signifies the other in a group or a series, the word ἑτερο⊠ means the other of two; for example, the other hand, the other eye and also the other sex or gender. In Greek language, we find 'ἑτερο' as a prefix in many terms. There remain only a few such terms in our language; for example, heterodox, heterogeneous, heterosexual. And, in some of these words, the meaning of 'hetero' has already lost its explicit reference to the number two, and instead refers to several or many, not two.

It is fitting to add that the term ἑτερο⊠ is not the only allusion to the number two. We also find the nominal and verbal dual form. For example, we could say in English: 'You two are beautiful and you will make it in the cinema'; 'The two of us are nice and we will leave Paris to help people in difficulty.' In these sentences, the dual form could be used for the verb, and also for the subject and the predicative adjective. It could also be used when there is reciprocity: 'We two love one another'. The dual form does not exist in all cases nor all tenses, and it is employed above all in Attica; in other areas of Greece, the plural is used as well as, and even more than, the dual form.

With regard to the term γενο⊠, I could note that originally this word refers as much to gender or sex as it does to generation and to other meanings. What I would like to emphasize is the fact that the meaning 'generation' or 'genealogy' has gradually supplanted the meaning of 'gender' or 'sex' for which the dual form can be used. I will try to suggest an explanation for this as well as for the disappearance of the morphological verbal form: the middle-passive or middle voice.

The middle-passive or middle voice does not have the meaning of our reflexive, which presupposes a split of the subject, but marks a certain return of the action upon the person. Thus, it can be partially reflexive – 'I wash my hands' – or reflexive in an indirect way, that is, the person acts in its own interest – to itself, for itself, from itself. For example, to obtain something for oneself, to remove a danger from oneself. 'To marry' can be expressed by the middle voice (above all for a woman). To return in oneself to draw energy, inspiration, wisdom is also expressed by the middle voice. Sometimes this form can be used when the action's return is on the whole person, but only if the body alone is concerned, or if it is a question of habits: 'I take a swim'; 'To dress oneself'. The middle voice is also used to express reciprocity: 'They love each other.'

I would like to stress the fact that the middle-passive or middle voice is a form that conveys both activity and passivity, and requires an involvement that is not merely mental. It can thus express a process of self-affection, and even of reciprocity, that neither simple active nor passive forms could convey. Now, in later cultures, coupling the opposites active and passive, and also using the reflexive, will substitute for the middle voice. However, if they presuppose a split of subjectivity, which is the norm in our tradition, they permit neither self-affection nor reciprocity.

I will also question the simultaneous disappearance of these terms, meanings and morphological forms, and that of the original representation of the feminine lips, of the female or feminine genealogy, and of a transcendental feeling which could be linked to such an evolution.

Self-affection in the masculine

The modalities of self-affection are not the same for man and woman, and nor are their lack or perversion the same.

For man, self-affecting is linked more with oneness, with the constitution of a world of his own, with the cultivation of this world to the point of its idealization. As I am not a male person, it is difficult for me to define what self-affection could be for a man; it would amount to substituting myself for him. I can only question a culture in the masculine. I note, then, that masculine subjectivity did not become differentiated enough from the maternal world. Thus the total relation that the male child has with his mother – the first other for him – has not been cultivated as such and, one could add, has not been submitted to a dialectic process. This has entailed several consequences:

1   It is through a division into body and mind, nature and culture, sensible and intelligible that masculine subjectivity has tried to emerge from an undifferentiated link with the first other.

2   More generally, it is through a logic of coupling
    opposites that masculine subjectivity seemingly
    separated off from its natural and affective origin,
    but such couplings became substitutes for difference
    between humans belonging to the two sexes and, first,
    between the mother and the male child.

3   Such a logic is thus ordered by genealogy, in particular
    in relation to certain of the couplings that are decisive
    for relational life: activity/passivity, love/hatred,
    nearness/distance, but also male/female and even I/
    other(s); and these couplings will have an influence
    on self-affection and the possible reciprocity between
    people, especially between two people.

4   This lack of differentiation from the maternal world
    prevents the definition of masculine subjectivity as a
    singular and, above all, a sexuate subjectivity.

5   Hence the fact that the relations between subjects in
    our culture have favoured relations amongst 'ones' or
    'somebodies' who are neutralized and can be substituted
    for one another

6   And the fact that affect is imposed on the subject from
    the outside and that it is more a source of imbalance
    than of harmony, or of enriching becoming; it has thus
    to be reduced by a turning back to homeostasis.

7   From this results the necessity of a closed mental world
    in order to protect oneself from affects

8   And the absence of subjective difference, first of all
of subjective sexuate difference; this has not been
recognized and cultivated as such with regard to the
mother, and, thus, difference has become in some way
only quantitative and, for example, referred to God as
the absolute other, the absolutely higher other.

9   The lack of cultivation of sensible immediacy and
its important impact on the relational becoming of
humanity.

The Western masculine subject has maintained an adhesion to
the maternal world, which he never submitted to a dialectical
process as such. Beyond the fact that this has paralyzed his
total becoming, notably his sensible and affective growth,
it has perverted his perception of truth. The separation of
intelligibility from sensibility does not solve the problem; rather,
it denies or represses it. This repression results in a veiling of the
perception of truth, which acts in every entering into presence.
It is through a certain sleep or dream that man approaches
the world. Pretending to unveil truth through his logos, by
fabricating truth or the world itself by himself, he increases
illusion instead of clarifying it. The world that man constructs
in this way is a dream world, and such a dream sometimes takes
a dramatic turn, as is the case today.

Furthermore, the world that man has built to supplant
his adhesion to the maternal world, to assert himself against
the mother, against participation in her world, has become a
screen, even a weapon, which intervenes between the masculine

subject and himself, and prevents any man from turning back to himself, in himself. Man has fallen into his own cultural trap. He is not only sheltered but also enclosed by his logos, becoming a prisoner of his own productions. Even in his attempts to return, or turn around or reverse, he is trapped by substitutes of his unconscious beginnings to which he remains blind. Going back home is perhaps possible after many efforts, after suffering great hardships. Turning back to the self is no longer possible. Without freeing himself from his adhesion to the other, the first other, man cannot return to his self. For lack of cultivation of the sensible relation with his mother – that is, of his first affects – man has cut himself off from experiencing his own self-affection.

The masculine culture as it is prevents man from turning back to himself. And even in his tradition, his country, his house, man is not 'at home.' The familiarity or intimacy that he feels is dependent on a web of habits or customs, but is not a real nearness. Wanting to master the alternation between near and remote through his logos, notably by transforming spatial distance into temporality, man has lost the possibility of approaching – things, the other(s), in particular the other of a different sex or gender. Familiarity has become for him the outcome of mastery, repetition, and even from confusion in worlds, unless it is mediatized by the other, in particular the feminine other. It does not result from a sharing of intimacy, not even with oneself. Self-affection has been confused with a dependence on the surrounding world, through which man believes he touches himself again. But the world that surrounds him is, in part, a substitute for a relation with the mother – a kind of placenta or construction for mastering the beginning of his life in the mother, employing an energy and a world common to the two. Culture, which intends to separate man from the maternal world, uses for its elaboration the relation with the mother herself.

In fact, the autonomy that man has gained is only apparent. Hence, the necessity for him of being and acting violently in order to enter into relations with the other: he tries to break the screen which divides him from everything and everyone. He attempts to demonstrate his competence, his know-how, while, or because, he is lacking in affective education, and even affective feeling, except at the quantitative level. What he feels is more or less intense but seems to be without nuances and singularities.

Not having yet worked out the first relation to the mother as an intersubjective relation, man merges with her in an energetic sharing, and merges with other men in a world made up of impersonal 'someones.' All men are supposed to share the same culture, the same values, and it is through such a uniformity that they should be affected from an outside – material or spiritual – without each being capable of affecting himself according to his own interiority. But without such an inner economy, affects have an immediate impact on energy; this increases and needs a release, or it spreads out and is wasted because of fear, dread and lack of concentration. That which provokes affects is often something that bursts into the closed horizon that man considers his world. That which affects him, in an immediate way, is strange to the man's world, at least to his supposedly own world. And the masculine subject is all the more immediately affected since he has not elaborated in himself a cultivation of self-affection. Thus any affect troubles his usual economy – his homeostasis, as Freud wrote. And this explains why any disturbance to his habits, anything that perturbs what is familiar to him – for example, the attraction or desire for the other or the coexistence with a foreigner – must end in a release, must become canceled in one way or another. The surplus of energy produced by the relation with the other as different cannot be stored and cultivated through the internalization of self-affection. It must be dissipated or invested in things or actions which are part of the surrounding world.

Western man has at his disposal very few markers, very little information to make his way along in relation with the other. Freud himself did not allude to a possible becoming in relation to sexual maturity, the so-called genitality. He spoke only about procreation, and about its necessity for the happiness of a marriage, the wife becoming able, in this way, to be a mother for her husband, and to give back to him his first lost relational world. Freud did not ask man to renounce his first relation with the mother or to sublimate it. On the contrary, he suggested that the wife has to substitute herself for the mother and become a mediation for the satisfaction of immediate male affects. The family will thus repeat on a small scale the cultural world based on the lack of differentiation between the subject and the maternal world. In any case, this constitutes the surroundings, including as other, which affect man without real self-affection internalized on his part.

In contrast to our culture, the relation with the mother has not been kept in the dark in all cultures, and it seems that the more it is eclipsed as natural origin and first human relation, the more it has influence on culture. This repressed dimension in our tradition has ultimately led to an overshadowing of another decisive natural dimension, that of sex or gender. The denial of the importance of the link with the mother has resulted in an emphasis on genealogy to the detriment of gender as sexuate identity. So the Greek word γενο⊠ increasingly came to express the vertical, and in some way hierarchical, genealogical dimension, and less and less the horizontal dimension of gender.

But emphasizing genealogy amounts to emphasizing natural reproduction and relations – a stress which is accompanied by many taboos in relation to nature – more than a relational cultivation of desire and love. A cultivation which asks us not to separate spirit from body, mind from affect. A cultivation which also requires each gender to care about its own self-affection, and to respect that of the other. Thus woman must not substitute herself for the mother of man, but has to cultivate her self-affection as a means of turning back to herself, and helping man in the discovery of his own self-affection – outside or beyond any sensible immediacy in their relations, be it intensely close or possessive.

Self-affection in the feminine

In contrast to man, woman is familiar with being two. A girl does not form a 'dyad' with the mother but a real duality. The similarity of their bodies and their psyches in their relational dimensions, including with respect to generation, protects them from merging into a unique entity. The two of the mother–daughter couple nevertheless does not suffice in securing an autonomous self-affection. Of course, the two of the mother–daughter couple – which does not amount to the mother–son dyad – can protect the girl from projecting all she has, all she is, onto a masculine subject. But the two of the mother–daughter relation runs the risk of perpetuating an original given situation, which is not yet cultivated as a possibility of returning to one's own self. The adhesion to the maternal world is different from that of the boy, but it can exist as a continuation or a repetition of an original situation, including a situation of dependence with respect to the mother and a given context.

Thus to reassert the value of female or feminine genealogy is certainly useful, above all in allowing woman to relinquish her dependence on masculine genealogy. However, going no further than genealogy could be a trap, an obstacle to the becoming of subjectivity. If dependence on masculine genealogy forces the girl or woman out of her own subjective becoming, going no further than female or feminine genealogy – in particular only in its natural dimension as is too often the case today – it generally amounts to an adhesion to a first relation which prevents girls and women from becoming wholly autonomous and accomplishing their subjectivity.

The self-affection of feminine subjectivity cannot stop with the mother–daughter couple. But it has more to do with duality than the self-affection of masculine subjectivity. I suggested that the morphology of the two lips could be a privileged place for woman to maintain a process of self-affection. Such a suggestion is supported by personal experience but also by a piece of cultural information. In the archaeological gallery of Syracuse in Sicily, there are many statues of the goddess Kore. Of course, I have listened to a guide emphasizing the statues of gods, and presenting all of these Kore as 'simple women,' perhaps only 'maidservants.' He did not know of the existence of the goddess Kore, even though her name was inscribed on the work. But the most interesting aspect was that these Kore do not have the same lips according to the century in which they were sculpted. The most ancient of them have closed lips, which touch one another and could be a good illustration of self-affection in the feminine. In later sculptures, the mouth is open and the lips no longer touch one another. And, finally, the mouth remains open and the lips are also distorted.

The story of Kore, taken from her mother, the great goddess Demeter, by the god of the underworld, is widely known. He raped her and kept her in the underworld – even changing her name – until her mother provoked a great famine on earth so that her daughter would be restored to her. The evolution of Kore's lips can be understood as a change in self-affection, which leads her to become dependent on an external instrument, or an other as instrument, for self-affecting, as a boy or a man is. What I have said about the virginity of woman as a condition for autonomy also is made clear. I allude to an ability to affect oneself through the lips touching one another without any external intervention or tool. It suffices that woman cares about gathering with herself, and remains concentrated on the affect which results from this touching, outside any other intervention or activity. It is interesting to experience what then happens, is felt, notably with respect to the two – that is the other and oneself – in a relationship. Such a gesture allows woman to come back to the self, within the self, and to respect the other, preserving a free space between the two.

How could women save this privileged place of self-affection in order to be able to return within themselves, to be faithful to their self, and to cultivate their own becoming – a necessary condition for entering into a dual relation with the other that does not amount to a repetition of the first link with the mother? How can women live a relation between two which does not confine itself to a 'dyad' or a coupling of opposites? This requires another culture to be elaborated. The cultivation of masculine subjectivity does not correspond to the same necessities, thus to the same values, as those of feminine subjectivity. Also, in the case of feminine subjectivity, a process of dialectization of sensible immediacy is necessary but in a different way from that which is needed by masculine subjectivity.

The feminine world is, by birth, more relational than the world of the boy, notably because of the privileged situation of the girl with respect to the mother, the same as the girl. This permits a duality of people from the very beginning, in particular through a relation to engendering different from that of the boy, of man. The girl knows what it means to beget, it is already a familiar experience for her through intuition or feeling. Turning back to birth, or beyond, does not seem a dangerous abyss to cover, to veil, as is the case for a masculine subject. The problem for feminine subjectivity is how to escape from what is only a natural state, at the level of birth but also at the level of relations with the other(s) – be they the mother, the lover, or the child, for example. What a woman has to do is to maintain an irreducible difference between the other and herself, while preserving her natural origin or roots. This can happen by arranging and keeping a transcendental dimension between the other and herself, particularly the other who belongs to a different origin – the masculine other. The matter, for a woman, is one of interposing between the other and herself a negative that cannot be overcome. Thus the transcendental would not be immediately deferred to the absolute 'you' of a God – who, in fact, then substitutes himself for the mother, the first other – as is too often the case for man in our culture. The transcendental must unceasingly intervene between the other and myself – the 'you' and the 'I' – turning the sensible immediacy of the relation into a cultivation of affect which can save the irreducibility between the other and myself, the insuperable difference between the two – the 'you' and the 'I'.

Self-affection needs to be two

A cultivation of self-affection by each one is what allows for the preservation and the becoming of attraction and desire between the two, by saving the difference between the two. It also permits an individual becoming thanks to a process of going back and forth between the self and the outside with regard to the self – another subject, object, or world.

A cultivation of self-affection seems to be lacking for us Westerners, in particular for man. Perhaps some mystics and artists have tried to approach it? But, even if they felt nostalgic for self-affection, most often they did not succeed in enjoying it. What might allow us to reach such a culture – beyond a cultivation of our own life, for example, through a practice of breathing – is a cultivation of the relationship between two subjects, a two different from the dyad formed by the mother and the male child. A cultivation of desire and love between the two sexes and genders is needed, not, first, as a sexual relation, but as a relation between two differently sexuate persons, whose self-affections are different and required as such. This 'two' can help man to leave a horizon built without a real differing from the mother's world – except through the neutralization of a 'someone,' a so-called neuter or neutral individual. It can also help him to escape the prison of loneliness and the dependence on the other or external objects for self-affecting. Desire, in fact, affects an energy internal to the subject and appeals to another subject, to reciprocity between two subjects. At least it should be so. Otherwise, it is not a question of desire, rather of instinct or drives. But only desire is really human.

Thus the relation between two is what can help man, and also woman, to gain access to an autonomous and internalized self-affection. At the grammatical level, one could say: to return to the middle-passive or middle voice as a way of internalizing, the middle-passive and not the opposition between active and passive: to affect/to be affected, which is perhaps fitting for the parent–child relationship. This pairing of opposites, which we have inherited from the first relation with the mother, has often been transferred between man and woman, with a reversal at the level of polarity: man becoming generally active with respect to woman, except, for example, in masochistic behaviour. And yet if the opposition active/passive has supplanted the middle voice, and somehow abolished it, such an opposition prevents us from cultivating our affects towards their internalization and cultural becoming, amongst others through reciprocity.

An anonymous world formed by 'someones' also leads to the passivity of each one in relation to affects coming from the outside, and does not allow the experience expressed by the middle voice, which requires us to pass from the outside to the inside of the self. A passage that only a relation between two permits, a relation that our tradition has deferred onto a unique God, whom humans would meet in another world.

Self-affection, expressed by the middle-passive or middle voice – and not an alternation between active and passive – is dependent on a relation between two: two who are different, even if they can form a whole, and who are not united by genealogy or hierarchy.

In earliest Greek culture, we still find the existence of the middle-passive or the middle voice, of the verbal and nominal dual form, and of a pronoun – ἑτερο⊠ – which expresses the relation in two or between two, two who are different, a difference that will later take on the value of subjection or opposition. The pronoun ἕτερος does not have the same meaning as ἄλλος, which is closer to our word: other. This ἄλλος – or other – in fact refers to any other and not to this other with whom I am in relation as two. The word 'other' is suitable for a world of 'someones' but does not favour the relation with an other who is different. It refers to a neuter or neutral, or better a neutralized, other, a kind of abstract individual about whom we can speak, but it would be difficult to meet as a concrete and living other. It seems that we could communicate between 'someones,' but we exchange only through a supposedly common world; and this does not yet reach a communication between subjectivities.

Our nostalgia for a return, amongst other things, to Greek culture could arise from wanting to return to our own self, within our own self, through self-affection. Cultivation of self-affection by woman as such seems to be the path which could allow man to leave the maternal world to reach his own self-affection.

Self-affection is neither secondary nor unnecessary. Self-affection – which once more does not amount to a mere auto-eroticism – is as much necessary for being human as bread is. Self-affection is the basis and the first condition of human dignity. There is no culture, no democracy, without the preservation of self-affection for each one.

Self-affection today needs a return to our own body, our own breath, a care about our life in order not to become subjected to technologies, to money, to power, to neutralization in a universal 'someone,' to assimilation into an anonymous world, to the solitude of individualism.

Self-affection needs faithfulness to oneself, respect for the other in their singularity, reciprocity in desire and love – more generally, in humanity. We have to rediscover and cultivate self-affection starting, at each time and in every situation, from two, two who respect their difference, in order to preserve the survival and the becoming of humanity, for each one and for all of us.